Walking the Path Where the Ghost Cows Live:

Honouring the Landscape of Grief

Tricia E. Bratton

Dear Anita
Thank you for your lovely friendship
Tricia

Dedication:

To my beloved husband, Stanley Jan Kukalowicz, who filled my life with immeasurable riches—may he rest in peace;

And to the Manchester Buddhist Centre Sangha, who lifted me when I could not stand—

may you all be well, and happy, and free from suffering.

Contents

Acknowledgments - - - - - 6

Prologue - - - - - 8

On The Seventh Day - - - - 10

PART ONE: Autumn

The Guest House, by Rumi - - - - 14
  1. Flight from Grief - - - - 15
  2. The Bench - - - - - 19
  3. Left Behind - - - - - 21
  4. A Thankful, Angry Heart - - - 25

PART TWO: Winter

Kindness, by Naomi Shihab Nye - - - 29
  1. Snow, Wind, Water, Rock - - - 32
  2. Simple Gifts - - - - - 35
  3. Broken Open - - - - - 38
  4. Layers of Loss - - - - 41
  5. Winter's Snow - - - - 46
  6. A Cuppa Tea - - - - 49
  7. The Monk's Room - - - - 52
  8. There Are Places I Remember - - 55
  9. Living Perpetually in Fear - - - 58

PART THREE: Spring

1. Turning Back the Clock - - - 62
2. Tender Touch - - - - 66
3. Ashes to Ashes - - - - 69
4. By the Sea, on My Own - - - 73
5. To Everything, There is a Season - - 77
6. Reach Deep, Find Warmth - - - 82

PART FOUR: Summer

1. Nero's Cry - - - - 86
2. Life Piles Up - - - - 90
3. This, Too, Shall Pass - - - 94
4. As Memories Fade - - - - 97
5. Making it to the Top - - - - 100
6. Grief Like a River - - - 104
7. Without Him in it - - - - 108
8. Enough - - - - - 111
9. Walking the Path Where the Ghost Cows Live 115
10. Back When My Heart was Pure - - 118

PART FIVE: Autumn
    1. Embracing the Silence - - - 124
    2. Living on Memory Lane - - - 128
    3. Pockets of Loss - - - - 131
    4. Searching for Stan - - - - 135
    5. The Things We Carry - - - 138

Epilogue: Honouring Grief, Honouring Stan - 143

Acknowledgments

Thanks go to the following publishers of two poems reprinted as a part of this book:

"Kindness" from *Words Under the Words: Selected Poems* by Naomi Shihab Nye, copyright © 1995. Reprinted with the permission of Far Corner Books.

And "The Guest House" by Rumi, and translated by Coleman Barks—reprinted here with the permission of the translator.

I have had many fellow travellers through this grief journey, which is not yet, and will never be, completely finished. I wish to acknowledge, first, Soaring Spirits International and Michelle Neff Hernandez, its founder, who invited me to become Monday's Writer for the blog, Widow's Voice. Michelle and the many volunteers at Soaring Spirits International work tirelessly to uplift and support widows (and widowers) throughout the world, of which the blog is an integral part.

I would like to acknowledge the many friends, neighbours and family members who have held onto me through this harrowing journey—from the members of my study group who have been with me every step of the way, encouraging me to reach, and grow, and giving me room to grieve, to the many friends in the US who have stood with me, via internet and phone calls, to my family—brothers, cousins, auntie, and niece, to Stan's friends, Stan's sisters, and Stan's children, who have continued to reach out to me while in the midst of their own grief.

I would like to thank my Dharma teachers, the many wise and brave women and men from the Triratna Buddhist Order, who bring us the Buddha's teaching through their classes, spiritual friendships, retreats, and writings, and who inspire me, through their practice and example, to live a life based on simplicity, generosity, and kindness.

A humble bow and great thanks, too, to Mr. Matthew New, who I do not know, personally, but who is a Triratna Sangha member in Birmingham, and who generously agreed to help me create this book.

I would like to acknowledge my children, Desmond Bratton and Ashley Frith, who flew in from New York to be at my side the moment I phoned them with the news of my husband's death. I am so thankful that they are a part of my life, and I hope they know how much I cherish them.

Prologue

The details of the road that led me to this loss are illuminated within the essays that form this book, but I will briefly summarise them, here: In February, 2011, I met a man who would change my world—Stanley Jan Kukalowicz. He lived in Glossop, England, and I, in London, but we were drawn together and fell in love—he, a British gentleman from the north, and I, an American Ex-Pat transplanted to London in 2009. I called it synchronicity, fate—what else could it be? How could two people with such different backgrounds and living 200 miles apart find each other and be such a perfect fit? But Stan did not believe in such things. He just said we were lucky, and advised me to leave it at that.

We were married in November of 2012, and I moved to Glossop to live with him. And in June, 2014, Stan collapsed and died, while walking hand in hand with me outside the funeral chapel, having just said goodbye to his son.

The first essay in this collection was written seven days after his death. It was read at both of his funeral services. The following essays were written as part of a blog called Widow's Voice. I wrote an essay each week for 52 weeks, reflecting upon the hills and valleys and turns and twists of my grief journey. I shared these posts with the widowed community, but also with family and friends. Many who read these posts told me that reading them brought them comfort, helped them to reflect upon their own journeys through grief and loss, and helped them to remember Stan.

So I decided to collect the best of them into a little book. Most of the profits from this collection will be donated to a bursary fund that was set up in Stan's name, to help people who couldn't otherwise afford it to attend Buddhist retreats.

To those who buy this book, thank you. Thank you for helping to preserve my husband's memory, and for honouring his generosity by contributing to the bursary fund. I hope my words bring you comfort. I hope they help you remember to treasure your loved ones. I hope they bring you some measure of peace.

On the Seventh Day

My beloved husband is dead. There are no other words to describe it.

Waves of grief followed by moments of laughter. Layers of memory stained with loss. Feeling him just beyond my reach. Outpourings of love from all corners of this wild, expansive area he cherished—those who wear his imprint from years of friendship, or those he touched with a momentary exchange over a cup of tea. The spirit of him wafting through these gentle hills.

Where do I go, now? And what do I do with myself? I had these thoughts, even before I lost him. Somehow I knew that our time together was short, that I would outlive the gift of his presence, that one day, I would be alone, again. I never dreamt it would be so soon.

Perhaps I'll learn Italian and find a cottage on a southern beach. Perhaps I'll pull out my worn, neglected hiking boots and train to tread the Appalachian Trail. Perhaps I'll put my words to use.

But today, I am here, in this bed we shared, his car parked on the road outside my window. Today, I sit, with the thwarted plans, the lost years of us, our teasing banter, our warmth, our mutual admiration, our easy ways.

I will miss him, the way he danced around the room when he was happy, his mispronounced words, his love for this world and the people he met, all the tiny pleasures he relished, his recognition of the beauty contained in this painful and delicate life.

I do not have an answer for this loss. I cannot ascribe to it any meaning—why some of us get to grow old together with all of our children beside us, get to share our lives with our siblings, to enjoy our parents into their old age. Why others of us suffer one loss after another, watch our loved ones topple, one by one, year by year, like bowling pins.

But I do know this: the world goes on. In the midst of my deepest sorrow, I awakened this morning. I watched the sun perch between the sloping hills my husband loved. I crept down the stairs and made myself a warm drink. I took up this paper and pen.

Despite the suffering, mine and that of others, the world is still here. What choice do I have, but to shake hands with it?

Autumn

The Guest House
By Rumi

Translated by Coleman Barks

This being human is a guest house.
Every morning a new arrival.

A joy, a depression, a meanness,
some momentary awareness comes
As an unexpected visitor.

Welcome and entertain them all!

Even if they're a crowd of sorrows,
who violently sweep your house
empty of its furniture,
still treat each guest honorably.

He may be clearing you out
for some new delight.

The dark thought, the shame, the malice,
meet them at the door laughing,
and invite them in.

Be grateful for whoever comes,
because each has been sent
as a guide from beyond.

Flight From Grief

How can I describe the strange set of circumstances that brought me here, from North America to Northern England, with its sloping, green hills, its mossy, stone walls, to this terrace house, built in 1889, to live the life that my husband gave to me?

I came from Florida to work in London, in a sort of flight from grief. I had lost my sister and then my mother, there, within eleven months of each other, both through lingering illnesses, and the pain of those losses sent me in search of a different life. I responded to an international recruitment of Social Workers to live and work in the UK, and, six months after my mother's death, in May of 2009, I arrived at Gatwick Airport, with two suitcases and a broken heart.

For months I covered over my grief, hiding it behind the flurry of concentration it took to negotiate living in a foreign land. I was intrigued by this new place, dazzled by its theatre, overwhelmed by its transport system, excited by the art museums and history museums, enamoured with the wealth of talent and the breadth of history in this country I now call home. I had much to do and see and learn. But I was not good at reaching out to others, and making connections in such a polite and formal society was not an easy task. It was a busy but lonely life.

The man that became my husband, Stanley Jan Kukalowicz, attended a Buddhist Centre in Manchester, from the same tradition as the South London Centre that I attended, and we came to know each other through our practice, there. We traded emails and phone calls for a couple of months.

Once, about a month after we had been communicating, I awakened in the morning to an email that contained a poem by Rumi and a picture of a sunflower.

How many 60 year old men read poetry and admire flowers?

I wanted to know this man.

We met. I held his hand at the Manchester train station, and looked into his clear, blue eyes. At 5 foot 4 inches, he was almost the same height as me, a rarity. Already we seemed a perfect fit. On our first date, he drove me through the bustling streets, past the red buildings of Manchester's inner city, to the Buddhist Centre, a beautiful building of wood and brick. Everyone knew him there, and greeted him warmly. We sat in silence before the shrine, the sweet smell of incense smoke twirling toward the ceiling.

He cooked me a meal, we talked, laughed, shared, and spent the entire weekend together. And the one after that. And the one after that—until our weekends became weeks and vacation times and grabbing every precious moment together that was possible for two people living and working 200 miles apart.

He shared his vibrant, colourful world with me—Sunday dinners in country pubs tucked into quiet corners at the end of winding roads, long drives throughout this vast and stunning landscape he loved, a large and robust family—six children, four sisters, three grandchildren, a host of lifelong friends. Music and dance. Humour and joy. He was comfortable with who he was. He was grateful for his life. He was peaceful and content.

We married on the 17th of November, 2012, and set about building a life. I moved into his home, found work, made a place for myself, and settled into my plan to grow old with the man I loved.

We overcame anxieties and conflicts and sadness, too. Merging the lives of two people who had traversed through many years and been hurt in other relationships had its challenges. He had some health problems, as did I. In April, 2014, he spent five days in hospital with an infection, and his recovery was slow and arduous. He lost a good friend, earlier in the year, another good friend had suffered a heart attack, and he was beginning to feel his age.

I had ties in America, a son I needed to visit, and this, too, put a strain on our relationship. We could not afford for both of us to go to America each year, so I went, on my own, in the summers, to visit my boy. In May, he graduated from university in upstate New York, and performed a senior recital, and I felt I needed to be there. My separation from Stan at this tender time was difficult, and far too long. We missed each other, terribly. I vowed not to be away from him for so long, again.

Five days after I returned from America, the police came to our door to tell us that one of Stan's sons had been found dead. He was 39. We spent the next two weeks swimming in grief and shock. We made funeral arrangements, notified his brothers and sisters and other relatives, cleaned out his flat. Stan was tired, and distant. I chalked it up to the exhaustion that comes with such a deep and tragic loss. I tried to console him, and give him space. I didn't know how to make it better. We were intent on getting through the day of his ceremony, hoping, then, to begin to heal. Gavin's funeral was set for the 9th of June.

On that day, after Stan had said goodbye to his son in a moving tribute that left everyone in tears, he walked hand in hand with me outside the chapel, looked into my eyes, and collapsed to the ground.

CPR, defibrillator, paramedics, rescue attempts.

Ambulance, A&E, more defibrillation, more CPR.

Flat line.

Shock, sorrow, wailing, disbelief.

Dead.

He brought me into his vibrant, colourful world, and left me in it.

Nearly five months later, I am still in shock. Except when I'm not. Except when the reality of his absence sends me to my knees. Each night that I arrive home and there is no one to pick me up from the train station. When I put my key into a darkened door. When I reach for him in our bed and find an empty place, instead. When I chase away the silence with television and internet.

These hills carry his spirit. I feel him everywhere. Sometimes they bring me comfort. Sometimes I want to run away from them, move to a different part of the world, like I did before, to make another flight from grief.

But I won't. It doesn't work, anyway, this running. I love these quiet, windy places, surrounded by stone, dotted with sheep. This is where he is. And I don't want to leave him behind.

This time, I'll face my loss.

The Bench

From the first time I met him, Stan spoke to me of his impending death. Not that he dreamt it would be happening anytime, soon. He just seemed to have a keen awareness of the one, inescapable fact of life we all share—that we will one day die.

Perhaps it was his witnessing of the untimely death of a close friend that kindled his awareness. Perhaps it was his Buddhist practice that brought him such a deep understanding of the precarious nature of our time on this earth.

I don't know. I only know that the possibility of death was always at the forefront of his consciousness, and it informed the way he lived his life.

He appreciated his days—even the smallest things—a good cup of tea, a rabbit hopping up a hill, the sound of rain on our roof, a chance encounter with an old friend on the High Street.

He didn't waste time on unimportant things—holding grudges, for instance, even against those who had done him great harm. Minor irritations, like traffic. He once phoned me from the motorway, on his way to London, having been stuck in traffic for two hours. His concern was not with himself, but with the persons who had probably been injured in an accident.

He had more patience than anyone I have ever known.

The first weekend we spent together, Stan took me to the summit of Monks Road, a street with ancient, Roman roots. The Monks of Baskingwerk Abbey walked this road in the 12th century, bringing their goods to market in the village below.

We stepped to the edge of a grassy hill, overlooking Manchester on one side, and Glossop on the other. The lights of the city cast an eerie glow on the dark, starless sky.

"I come up here when I am not feeling right," he told me. "I look out over these hills, and realise how insignificant my problems are. When I die, this is where I want my ashes scattered," he said. "I want others to come here, after I'm gone, to recognise that, too."

I remember feeling so privileged that he had shared his sacred spot with me. I felt honoured that he trusted me, already, with his eternal place.

When he died, I discovered that I was not the privileged, trusted person I had envisioned, after all. He had brought almost everyone he knew up to that spot, at some point, giving each of them a similar speech.

He made certain we were very clear about the location of his final resting place.

I will take him there, but not just yet.

For now, I have his ashes here with me. They are heavy and dense, settled inside a large, round tube.

I have made him a little shrine, in the bedroom, with our picture above it, and it is a comfort to me, this cardboard barrel of bones and ash. It is what I have left of the body I loved.

In the spring, his friends and family will gather to scatter them there, in the nutty grasses, surrounded by his beloved hills.

I've decided to install a bench, too, at his sacred spot.

I hope the bench I place in memory of my husband will bring comfort to those who knew him. I hope they will come to the summit of Monks Road and sit with him awhile, leave a flower, have a chat.

I hope the view will help them to remember how small their problems are

I hope it will help them to remember him.

Left Behind

Two years ago, on November 17th, 2012, my husband and I were getting married. It was a chilly autumn day, and the rain paused long enough for us to gather at the registry office in New Mills for our simple, beautiful ceremony. Later, we brought close friends and family to our local pub, The Beehive, for a reception and delicious dinner.

No one from America was with me at my wedding, and Stan knew I would be missing their presence, so he put together a slideshow with pictures of them and played it on a screen at the party we held later in the evening. It was a sweet and thoughtful gesture, his attempt to bring my old world into our new, shared life.

Eighteen months later, we gathered at The Beehive, again, to mourn my husband's passing.

All of Stan's family and friends were there. But my son and his girlfriend were the only ones who could come, on such short notice, from America, to be with me.

Our second anniversary falls on a Monday, this year, and, though I knew others would remember it, I didn't feel I could ask them to take time away from their working lives to sit with me on that day, to help me commemorate it, and I did not want to face it on my own.

So I decided to come 'home,' to rest, to be surrounded by the people with whom I was raised, and to try to heal a little bit. I'll be here for Thanksgiving, too, that distinctly American holiday, a day I don't even pay attention to, when I am in England.

I am here in Indiana, at my brother's house, who lives on the street where we grew up. Yesterday I walked down that street and recalled the names of each of our neighbours as I strolled past their homes. I walked through the subdivision where my childhood home once stood, and looked up at the pine trees that I used to climb when I was little. I walked down the hill to my muddy creek, a creek I spent a lot of time with, as a child, skipping rocks across its waters.

The world I inhabit, when I come to America, is so much different than the world I have in England. It is a known world, here, with wide, spacious streets, giant yards and houses, chain stores and franchise restaurants, the familiarity of fifty-two years of living. And though I love the life I have in England, and I cherished my life with Stan, I settle into the rhythms and ways of America very easily when I am here, and there is a certain comfort in it.

It is a world that, aside from two, steaming weeks in May of 2012, my husband never knew.

Sitting here, on this cold, snowy, Indiana morning, I wonder if I did the right thing, coming here to spend our second anniversary. I can't feel his presence here. Stan and England feel so very far away.

I feel like I have left him behind.

Six months ago, in May, 2014, I was back in America for my son's graduation from a Master's Program in Music. Stan had not been well, having only been in the hospital a few weeks before my scheduled trip, but he was well enough to return to work, and so I decided to go ahead with my plans to be there for my son. I kissed my husband goodbye at the Manchester airport on May the 2nd, 2014.

My days in New York were filled with activity. We hiked around the falls and gorges there; I attended my son's graduate recital, beamed with pride at his many accomplishments, met up with some old friends who lived nearby.

Through the wonder of technology, I was able to connect, often, with Stan, via FaceTime. But the difference in time zones made planning for those connections difficult, and we did not always get to chat. I was immersed in the American world I knew so well, and did not always find time for my husband. I knew we would be together soon, when I returned to him in England, and my focus was on my son.

When I returned to England, Stan told me he had felt left behind.

He could not share in my world and he missed me sharing in his. I remember that I became a bit defensive, upon hearing this, and I was not as kind to him as I should have been in response. I told him I had so little time with my son, and that sometimes I felt torn between the two worlds. I did not want to have to choose one over the other. Both worlds were important to me.

Three weeks after I returned home from America, my husband was dead.

Inevitably, when someone dies so suddenly, loved ones pour over missed opportunities, experience longings and regrets.

I cannot put into words how much I regret those last few weeks. I feel terrible that I spent two weeks away from him when he was not completely well. I wish I had taken time to connect with him, on those days we did not talk, that I had been more mindful of his need to hear from me. I wish I had known how short our time would be.

If only I had known.

But I didn't. I thought we would have many more years together. I planned to work harder to integrate my two worlds in the future, and we talked of taking the next trip to America, together. I hoped that my husband would come to understand my American life, eventually, and come to share it, with me.

There wasn't time for all of that. And sitting here, amongst the familiar voices and sounds and surroundings of my childhood, I must try to forgive myself. It is not easy to live between two worlds. I had only lived my life in England, with my husband, for a few short years. I got swept up in America every time I came here.

It was only natural that I would.

Today, the 17th of November, 2014, two years after our wedding, I will try to bring my husband's memory here with me. I will look over our wedding photos, light a candle for him, help those here to know him a little bit.

I know Stan would be telling me, in his kind, gentle, way, to forgive myself, to let go of regrets. He knew that I loved him, and that I would never, truly, leave him behind.

And I have to hold onto that.

A Thankful, Angry Heart

It is the week of Thanksgiving, and all around me there is the message to be grateful, to be thankful for what I have, and to count my blessings.

I am thankful for many things—my brothers and their families, who made sure I got to visit them, my cousins and aunts and uncle, who made special efforts to see me while I am here, my son and his girlfriend, who travelled from faraway places to support me in my visit.

I am thankful for Stan's family and for the beautiful part of the world he gave to me. I am thankful for my spiritual community, and for Stan's friends and neighbours, the loving people who have supported me in the aftermath of his death.

But today, I am feeling tired and sad and angry. People say it is not possible to be angry and grateful at the same time. Perhaps those people have not faced great loss. This grief journey has taught me that I can carry a multitude of feelings, often conflicting, at once—gratitude and anger, joy and sorrow, hope and despair. We hold all of these within us, and try to function at the same time, to smile and interact and focus and pretend that we are fine, so that those around us won't worry. No wonder we are exhausted.

I am thankful that I met and loved this man.

Lately, I have pondered this question—if someone were to tell me that I was going to meet and fall in love with a man who would change my world, but that I would only have him for a short time, would I have risked it? Would I have taken the plunge, knowing I would face such deep sorrow? I like to think I would.

But maybe not. Maybe I would have been too afraid. Maybe I would have chosen to stick with my safe, predictable life, in order to spare myself this grief.

So it is probably a good thing that I could not have foretold our fate, before we met. I would have missed so much. I would have missed knowing him.

The truth is, on this day, I am angry that he is gone. I feel cheated. I found the love of my life, and I was meant to grow old with him. And in 3 ½ short years, he was taken from me, at the drop of a hat. Before my very eyes. I don't know how to be grateful for that.

Some people claim that everything happens for a reason, but I can't believe it. I gave up on that belief when my mom and sister died. I can no longer conceive of a higher power that has some grand plan for us. How could such a cruel fate as this be part of some grand plan?

There is no sense in it.

I prefer to believe that all things rise and fall, and that all beings are part of this ever-changing flux. Sometimes it feels so random. But it is just the way of the world. There is not a lot of easy comfort in this belief. That is why we practice acceptance.

Some things are easier to accept than others. And it may take me a few more months or years to reach that place of acceptance with Stan's death. At the moment, I rail against it. I hope that, at some point, I will come to a place of peace.

Stan had a thankful heart. Every day, he woke up thankful. He would draw the curtains open and praise the weather, even if it was grey and wet. He joyfully accepted the cups of tea I brought him.

Even on the last day of his life, the day of his son's funeral, when he found it difficult to get out of bed, he thanked me for his morning cup of tea.

I am angry and I am thankful. I am thankful for the time I had with him. I am angry he is gone. I hold both of these things in my heart.

Winter

Kindness

Naomi Shihab Nye

Before you know what kindness really is
you must lose things,
feel the future dissolve in a moment
like salt in a weakened broth.

What you held in your hand,
what you counted and carefully saved,
all this must go so you know
how desolate the landscape can be
between the regions of kindness.
How you ride and ride
thinking the bus will never stop,
the passengers eating maize and chicken
will stare out the window forever.

Before you learn the tender gravity of kindness
you must travel where the Indian in a white poncho
lies dead by the side of the road.
You must see how this could be you,
how he too was someone
who journeyed through the night with plans
and the simple breath that kept him alive.

Before you know kindness as the deepest thing inside,
you must know sorrow as the other deepest thing.
You must wake up with sorrow.
You must speak to it till your voice
catches the thread of all sorrows
and you see the size of the cloth.

Then it is only kindness that makes sense anymore,
only kindness that ties your shoes
and sends you out into the day to purchase bread,
only kindness that raises its head
from the crowd of the world to say
It is I you have been looking for,
and then goes with you everywhere
like a shadow or a friend.

Snow, Wind, Water, Rock

It is almost Christmas, and I have spent most of the last ten days on my own, in silence. At times, I have thought that I should make an effort to visit with people, make connections, socialise. I just don't seem to handle it well. Even a short trip to the shops on the High Street brings me to tears—couples hand in hand, brightly coloured lights, fresh trees for sale, Santas in the windows, ribbons and bows, carols blasting through the speakers—all this celebration and excess is out of sync with the way I feel, inside. I am awkward around people.

I don't know how to act. What do I say? What greetings do I employ? Merry Christmas? Happy Holidays? I don't even want to think about the New Year. I want to crawl under the covers until it is all finished.

The one time my world makes sense, these days, is when I walk, alone, into the hills. I set my boots onto a muddy path, my face exposed to the biting wind, and watch my breath stream in and out. I hear birds rustle in the trees above me. I see rabbits hop into the underbrush. I take note of the droplets of water, hanging, like tears, on naked branches. I feel the rain, sleet and snow pelt against my skin. I put one foot in front of the other. I don't have to worry, or plan, or think. I only walk, and breathe.

When I am outside, among the elements, it feels that perhaps I do have a place on the planet. I find a sliver of hope that, perhaps, one day, I will heal.

I am currently in the midst of reading my third book about thru-hiking the Appalachian Trail. This trail, which spans 14 states from Georgia to Maine, is 2,172 miles in length and takes six months to complete. I obsessively research the proper equipment to purchase, which parts of the trail are the hardest, which shelters are best, what critters I may encounter on the trail, both irritating and dangerous. This, I do, while finding it difficult to venture out of the house, some days.

Perhaps my walking this trail is a wild fantasy that will never be fulfilled. I have a mortgage to pay, and a job to go to, and a need for comfort. I am not sure this almost 58-year-old body could even withstand such an endeavour.

Yet, there is a part of me that wants to mark this monumental change in my life in a monumental way. It doesn't feel right to have gone through the trauma of watching my husband die and to return to my regular, mundane existence—to trudge to work and to shop in stores and to pretend that I am the same. I am not. Nothing will ever be the same.

I want to have an outward expression, beyond these words, of the depth of my grief.

I read somewhere that it is a Jewish tradition to tear one's clothing, over one's heart, after a death. I want to do this—tear my clothing, beat my chest, rub my face with ashes, shave my head—something, anything, to mark this sorrow.

I loved the life I had here, with him, walking these hills, Sunday drives, our nights together. I still love the place where I live and the world he gave to me—stone walls and terrace houses, the remnants of century old mills, stately churches and castles, the beautiful, windswept moors, the ever changing landscape—shadow and light, snow and wind, water and rock.

But it is wrong to proceed with this life as if nothing has changed. I feel a need to purge, to cleanse, to let go of the me that was, before his death, to slough off the old me, to make myself anew.

I don't know if I will have the heart and the strength and the courage to do this thing. But, I have done it before. I have changed my entire life. The last time I lost two people, my mother and sister, I moved from Florida to England. This move is what brought me to my husband.

Now he's gone. And my world has, once again, shifted. And I can't continue to walk around like it hasn't.

Simple Gifts

On Tuesday, I am going away for four days on a Buddhist Retreat. I will spend Christmas Eve, Christmas Day, and Boxing Day there. This is my first Christmas without Stan, and it seemed the best way for me to let the holiday pass, as much as possible, without notice.

I won't be celebrating Christmas this year, but I have wrapped some simple gifts for the people who have held me up when I felt I would surely crumble. Stan's friends and family have found their way through their own grief to reach out to me and remind me that I am in their thoughts and hearts. I hope my small token of appreciation will help them to know how important their generosity of time and presence has been to me.

My Buddhist sangha, my spiritual community of friends and teachers, has been the rock that I have leaned on through these last few months. I am not certain I would have survived without them. They made sure that my husband's memorial services were meaningful and beautiful. They generously gave of themselves in those first few days and weeks, when I could not eat or sleep or think. They lit candles in his honour and placed his photo in the reception area and on the shrine, next to the Buddha. In the months since his death, when most people have returned to their daily lives, they continue to allow me to express my sadness, and they are not afraid to speak his name.

I sit in meditation most days, but some days, I am afraid to make space for what will come, that whatever it is underneath all my busyness and chatter might overwhelm me, if I allow it to surface. I sit at home, on my own, or meditate with friends at the Centre.

When I make time and space to sit in silence, not planning or doing or thinking, the sadness inevitably erupts, from a place deep within, from the pit of my stomach, and, most often, I cry. It is not something I can control, and I think it is best that I don't try to control it. It feels healing to sit quietly, before the shrine, with all that I am, at that moment, and to let the tears come. I breathe with the tears, and let them fall onto my cushion, not moving to quell them or rub them away.

Particularly, during our ritual pujas, in which we chant and recite ancient sutras and sacred texts, I am moved to tears. The aroma of incense, the trail of smoke rising to the ceiling, the glow of candlelight, the harmonies of chanting, the people in my sangha bowing in humble reverence before the shrine—all of these elements combine to move me beyond my thinking head and toward my heart. It is then, when I allow the controls I place upon myself to slip away, that my sorrow arises. I remember Stan and feel his absence from our sangha. I feel the emptiness he left behind.

Not long ago, our sangha gathered to celebrate one of several festivals we hold throughout the year, and we concluded our day with a ritual puja. Little tea candles lined the pathway from the back of the room to the shrine, and the chanting was hauntingly beautiful, that night. I remembered Stan, and I let the tears come.

People walked toward the Buddha with gifts of flowers and incense, offerings to lay upon the shrine. I closed my eyes and deepened my breath. When I opened them, I found that a flower had been laid at my feet. An Order member had seen my sadness, and, when taking his offering to the Buddha, decided to give the flower to me, instead.

His gift of the Buddha's flower meant the world to me. It meant that my sorrow was witnessed and accepted. It meant that my grief could be held and responded to and met by others.

I am blessed by the compassion and presence of my friends in the sangha, my spiritual home. My heart is soothed by the simple gifts they bring to me—an invitation to share a walk together, a conversation and a cup of tea, a thoughtful card in memory of my husband, the Buddha's flower, laid at my feet.

Broken Open

"There is a crack, a crack in everything. That's how the light gets in."
Leonard Cohen

My heart has been broken by the death of my husband. It feels unfair that he left us so soon. We were just beginning our lives together. We were good companions and the best of friends. He had children and grandchildren who needed his guidance. He was on the cusp of transforming his life.

When my heart feels broken, I draw the curtains and shut the door. I circle the wagons and hide in the middle. I curl into a ball and turn off the lights.

Then I remember how Stan softened me. My heart is broken because my love was real. I don't want his death to harden me again.

Stan's life and death changed me forever. I am not the person I was before.

I once placed great value on my opinions. I thought them morally superior to those who opposed me. I was a big fan of political debate, and always certain to have the last word.

But I've lost my desire for conflict. My opinions don't seem to matter, much. When people were shouting, Stan urged me to see the pain and fear behind their anger. "It's only a view," he'd tell me. He taught me to lean toward kindness. He showed me how to meet their pain with love.

I used to fancy myself a misfit. I revelled in my uniqueness. I was not like all the others, I thought. I was deep, and complicated, and misunderstood. I felt weird and awkward around people. An outcast. Alone.

Now, I search for what connects us. I see that we are all born and we all will die. I knew this before, but now I have witnessed it, and it's made me different. I see how we feel lost and afraid, and how we cover our fears with words and certainty and attempts at control. If we are lucky enough to live very long, we will all know whiskers, and wrinkles, and achy joints. We have moments of joy, and glimpses of peace. We all fear losing our loved ones.

His death taught me to remember these things.

People's ways used to grate on my nerves. I was easily offended, and good at finding fault. This one drank too much, that one talked too loudly, this one chewed with his mouth open, that one's voice quivered when she spoke. I took their ways as a personal affront.

I'm less prone to irritation these days, and quick to forgive perceived slights. Each of us has our habits and defences, and we navigate this scary and shocking world the best we can. I am learning to let people be.

I used to be careful, and shy, and slow to warm, afraid I'd be rejected, and look a fool. Then Stan died, and I found that time is short. We could be gone in an instant. We could be cut right down. It's made me lose my filter. Now I want to celebrate the people I love.

I have a tremendous affection for those who knew Stan. My heart leaps for joy when I greet them. I am so grateful that they knew him and loved him, that they remember him, and miss him, too. He feels alive to me in their presence. I want to hug them and squeeze them. I think my exuberance scares them a little bit!

I spent four days last week on retreat in Shropshire, in a building of simple brick, set at the end of a long, dirt road. Thirty women gathered in this peaceful place, to meditate and study, to sit in silence and reflect. Freed from the disturbance of city lights and internet, immersed in spaciousness and quiet, I felt my heart open up.

On Christmas Eve, there was the sliver of the moon, and a hundred thousand stars across the sky, dancing with delight. I walked down a muddy path to sit before a rupa of Prajnaparamita, the mother of all the Buddhas, future, present, and past. Under that starry night, I let my sorrow rise, and I cried out to the heavens my loss of Stan. I felt the ground beneath my feet. I let the stars and rupa cradle me. I let the earth absorb my tears.

Back in my little room, I lay in darkness and listened to my breath. I stared at the stars outside my window, and I asked Stan to teach me kindness. He was so good at it. He put aside his petty quarrels and inner turmoil to tune in to the people around him. He knew how to show up in the way that they needed--a few soft words at the reception desk, a strong shoulder to lean on, a warm hand grasping theirs--a lift to the hospital for a poorly friend, an evening call to his young son at University, his "Daddy's Pasta," cooked for his children, stirred with love, in a giant pot.

My heart has been broken open by the death of my husband. I hope I can let his light shine through it.

Layers of Loss

I awakened this morning, on the last day of 2014, with the images of my mother and sister on my heart. They died 6 and 7 years ago, respectively, during the holiday season, and I realised I had done nothing, this year, to mark their lives and deaths—not a picture or a mention, anywhere. I have been so consumed with the loss of my beloved that memories of them sifted into the dusty corners of my consciousness.

It is said that people die as they lived, and, in my mother and sister's case, this saying surely rings true.

My sister became diabetic at the age of 14, and she defied all the rules that were set for her around it, as teenagers tend to do. Her blood sugars skyrocketed and plummeted throughout her life with frightening frequency, sometimes sending her into diabetic shock. As she aged, she began to build mountains of possessions around her, until the home she shared with my mother became a bunker, of sorts, with lumps of clothing and boxes of books lining the walls and stacked to the ceiling, a small pathway carved through the middle that the two of them could barely navigate their way through.

When she got sick, she sloughed off those possessions like a snake sloughs its skin, leaving them behind without a backward glance.

She died in Hospice House, with a cancer that spread through her body like wildfire, bumps and tumours poking out from her thighs to her shoulder blades, visible and painful to the touch.

Her last breaths were strained and rattled, interspersed with pleading moans.

My sister did not go gentle into that good night.

She left behind a son, a beloved granddaughter, some grandchildren she had yet to meet, an array of holiday hats and socks, and hundreds of people who cherished her wild and troubled spirit.

Her name was Debra, and she died on the 12th of December, 2007. She was 56.

I did not forget.

My mother was sweet, and small, and often afraid. I did not recognise her quiet strength until I learned to view her through the eyes of a mother, rather than those of an angry child. She lived in poverty for most of her life, first on a farm in Kansas, where she carried milk buckets through snow swept fields and pulled weeds from the garden in the hot summer sun, looking to the skies and pining for a bigger life than the one into which she was born. She worked hard in school and travelled a little before she met my father, whose charm and humour took her by surprise. He was a wise spirit, but he drank a bit and dreamed a lot, moving her from the poverty of the farm to a suburban deprivation that left her disconsolate and ashamed.

My mother did her best to tame the roller coaster life my father lived, and to help her four children settle somewhere near the ground. She canned vegetables in summer and made grape jelly in the fall, stoked the fire with coal when we had some, in winter, tacked scraps of carpet to splintered floors, and sent us to scouts and swimming lessons and bible school. She sang tenor in the church choir every Sunday, her low and haunting voice blending in harmony with those who stood in the forefront.

My mother had surgery to repair a hernia seven months after my sister died. The doctors cut a hole in her throat that left her unable to tell someone when she had to go to the toilet or to ask for a drink of water to quench her thirst. They left my mother without a voice. Speechless.

Later, when they plugged the hole, the experience had so traumatised her that she could not eat, and she became so malnourished that her feet swelled like puffer fish, and she couldn't remember if she had to pee, or where she was, or why she was still alive. The doctors put a tube up her nose and down her throat to feed her, then. She moved from the hospital to my home and back again, for four months, and when she lay in that hospital bed, she did not once ring the bell to ask for help. She did not want to disturb anyone.

My mother died at Hospice House, two doors down and eleven months from where she had watched her daughter take her last breath. My brother said that her breaths slowed quietly and when they stopped, he felt her spirit fill the room. My mother was tired of being voiceless. She was ready to leave the life that had, only occasionally, been kind to her.

She left behind two sons, a host of grandchildren and great-grandchildren, boxes upon boxes of photos and letters, sweet stories of her childhood, and a daughter with a shattered heart.

Her name was Bervelee Jean, but people called her BJ, and she let them, because it was easier to pronounce, though she never liked it, much. She died on the 15th of November, 2008. She was 82.

I did not forget.

My husband came into my life on a whirlwind, and we travelled our road together with passion and joy, joined by a seemingly boundless love. He invited me into his rich world of green hills, bathed by evening's light, and bordered by walls of stone, a bustling family of sisters and children and grandchildren, and a multitude of friends. He taught me about music and dance, patience and calm, and how to search out rabbits in the snow.

Now it is the 1st day of 2015, and I have moved into a new year without him in it. I try to believe that I will carry him with me into this new year, that I will bring him alive in how I open to the people around me, the way he did, in how I speak his name, when I think of him, in how I rejoice in the man that he was to all who are willing to listen.

But he is not here, in the physical realm, and I will never again be able to kiss him or wrap my arms around him or hold his warm, strong hand. And it makes me sad and sore with longing.

My husband died in a whirlwind, in an instant, walking out the door of the chapel at the funeral of his son. I wish it had been different. I wish we had time to say goodbye, to fluff his pillows, and soothe his pain, and wipe his forehead with a cool cloth. It would have been easier for us. But it would have been the worst way to die, for him. He lived his life, fully, and died without warning. Too soon. Far too soon.

His name was Stanley Jan Kukalowicz, and he died on the 9th of June, 2014. He left me with his beautiful family, a century old house, these striking hills, a thousand friends who loved him dearly, and the gift of a deep and expansive love.

He was 63.

I will not forget.

Winter's Snow

On this bleak, grey, England winter's day, I remember the comforting quiet of snow. Stan loved the snow. He would sit for hours by the window, watching it. When we first began to talk to each other, he told me that he wanted to move to the Northeastern coast of England, near Whitby, where he said they had a 'proper winter'. Proper winter? I had moved to England from the west coast of Florida, just a year before, and the bits of snow I had encountered in London, that year, were quite enough, for me, thank you. But he wanted to see more of it.

When he was a little boy, he told me, he used to cry when the snow melted. I will always remember that sweet image of him, as a child, wiping his tears as the snow disappeared into the boggy ground.

Today I understand his love of snow. It turns the grey days white with promise. It makes everything new again. Walking into the hills, the biting wind brushing my cheeks, I hear my footsteps crunch against the frozen ground. Bare branches glisten with ice droplets. Black crows hop and peck their beaks into the frost covered earth in search of food. Blessed sun warms the slick pathway climbing upward, past blanketed horses, their breath steaming from cold nostrils, past woolly sheep, huddled against stone fences, toward the summit, hidden by misty cloud. I could get lost up there. It wouldn't be a bad way to go.

When I was young, living in Montana, and contemplating ending my time on this earth, (which I did, often, in those days), I decided that the easiest way to go would be to climb to the top of some mountain, and wait for the cold to envelop me, wrapping me in its blue tendrils, until I couldn't feel a thing. I would just get sleepy, I thought, and pass peacefully away. Perhaps I'd stay frozen until spring, when some hiker would come across my mummified corpse. Or perhaps the animals would use me for food, and my sun-bleached bones would be all that they'd find. At least my life would have served some purpose, I thought. It was a twisted comfort for my tortured soul, back then.

These days, my grief is deep and all-encompassing. But I am not the tortured soul I was. As much as the loss of my beloved husband has broken me, I do not feel defeated. I have been softened by this experience. His death was tragic, true. I would not wish this pain on anyone. It is the worst thing that has happened to me. And it has made me tender-hearted.

Staying soft is difficult. My natural instinct is to protect myself from the prospect of further hurt and sorrow. Leaving myself open to others means I most certainly will feel the pain of loss, again. Perhaps not a loss that cuts so deeply. But pain and loss, nonetheless.

My husband understood the importance of staying soft. He knew deep sorrow. He experienced trauma and turmoil as a young lad. He used many salves, through the years, to bind and heal those wounds. But he did not let them make him hard and bitter. He used his sorrow to reach out to others. He had a deep empathy for those who suffered. He had seen much suffering, himself.

Today, I find a different kind of hope in winter's snow. I feel nurtured and warmed by its white blanket. I like to nestle into its silence. There's less frantic activity when snow closes in. People slow their pace. Buses and trains and planes come to a standstill. Folks stay home, and make space for their thoughts, and for each other.

When snow comes to my hills, I open the curtains, build a warm fire, and pour myself a hot drink from the kettle. And I remember him, up all night, seated at the window, snowflakes falling.

A Cuppa Tea

My husband was an Englishman, and loved his tea. I learned early that there is an art to making it, even though, to me, it seemed a simple process of teabag into cup. But no. Some like it strong, some like it weak. Some prefer it with milk, some without. Some like two sugars, some like one. To forget how guests like their tea, when they come to visit, is considered impolite.

My husband liked it weak. His was more like coloured water. Just a swipe of the teabag in the cup. Pour the boiling water from the kettle, swirl the bag around, take it out.

He wasn't particular about the type. He was a working class man. He didn't get snooty and insist on English Breakfast or Earl Grey. Although he did not fancy our Lipton's Tea when he was in America. He said our tea was rubbish.

When we first met, he stood over me and showed me exactly how he liked it. From then on, it became my job to make him his cups of tea. I would bring him his first cup in the morning, and set it on his bedside table before I went off to work. When I got home at night, and turned my key in the door, I could hear his voice as I opened it. "BooBoo? Is that you?" Invariably followed by, "Could you bring me a cup of tea?"

Most often, he would be upstairs in his man-cave, on his computer, playing music, writing, studying his dharma lessons. Scattered around him would be two or three or four cups. Did he not think to take one down, and use the same one each time, I used to think? I would bring him a new cup of tea, gather the other cups to take downstairs, and he would wrap his arm around my waist, pull me toward him, and thank me, always.

He drank a lot of tea. He must have found comfort in having a hot drink, even in summer. Our summers are not that hot, here in England, so a cup of tea never seemed out of order.

This meant he had to use the bathroom, a lot. On our road trips, (and there were many, in the short time we were together), we would have to make frequent stops so that he could use the toilet. Then we'd need to sit and have another cup of tea.

It used to irritate me, having to stop every hour or two for tea and toilet breaks. I was an American, after all, and we buy our coffee at the drive-thru, and drink it in a Styrofoam cup, while barrelling down the highway. We have many more miles to cover, on our road trips through America, and we think we need to get someplace, fast. No time to stop. Our lives are too driven to consider such a thing.

Stan liked stopping. He knew how to slow down. He liked to sit in a spot and watch people, smile, have a conversation, and maybe a little snack.

My husband. How I miss his calling for me when I turn my key in the door. Gathering his cups. His thank yous for that simple act of nurture.

I have the same box of tea bags I had when he died, seven months ago. No one to use them, now.

Perhaps I'll set my coffee habit aside, and learn to love tea. I'll pour it into the cup my husband's grandchildren bought me for Christmas. A quick swipe of the bag, swish it around, take it out.

Just the way he liked it.

The Monk's Room

Perhaps it is the frozen weather that has me frozen in my grief. I am not certain of the reason. I only know that, this week, I have felt the full weight of his absence. In eight days, it will be eight months since my husband died. It feels like a whole lifetime has passed, since he left us. It feels like it happened yesterday. I sit with both realities.

I have not altered much in this house that belonged to him. I don't have the heart to do it. The living room looks virtually the same as the day he walked out that door.

But I did redo the room where he spent most of his time, when he was alive. I made it into a guest room, should anyone from America decide to visit.

I never liked that room. It was always so messy, with his software and hardware strewn about, with its overgrown furniture, too big for the tiny space it inhabited. Now, it is tastefully furnished and everything fits. But it feels like a sterile place, without him in it.

I call it the monk's room, because it is small, with little space for possessions or frivolities. It is a simple room, and free from distractions. I have made a small shrine, in there, where I sit in meditation, some days, while the morning light streams through the window.

When we first met, Stan would sit at his computer and write emails to me, describing what he saw from that window. He loved the overgrown plants in the garden below, the vines growing over the sheds, creeping into the trees, providing a haven for birds and squirrels. Here is one of the emails he sent me, written on a sunny, spring day in 2012:

"Yet another beautiful day here in Glossop, where all around me new life is unfolding--birds attending to nests for their future fledglings, catkins on the silver birch being visited by

bees, unfurling leaves revealing their true identity, and the sun caressing the earth to energise all these wondrous and mystical things."

He loved sunny days, but he appreciated the rain, too. He understood the need for it. Here is an email he wrote me, earlier that spring, describing the rain:

"The rain is pitter pattering on the windowpane, creating an interesting beat. The rain will also wash all the salt and sand from my car, whilst building reserves to refresh living things, as the long hot sunny days arrive. This truly wondrous web of life we share."

I feel his presence in that room, more than anywhere else in the house. Sometimes I lie on the bed, in there, and talk to him. I can almost see him, in his dressing gown, his blue eyes fixed upon the intricacies of the natural world that he saw and described so clearly.

I like to look out the window, too, peering over the rooftops of the other terrace houses, toward the hills in the distance. Today those hills are blanketed in snow. He would have loved that.

The plants that he cared for in that room are dying. I don't know why. I have never been good with plants. He was a gardener. Growing plants came naturally to him.

I repotted one of them, thinking that perhaps the leaves were wilting because the pot was too small, but no. The leaves are still yellowing and turning crisp, then falling away.

I hate to look at those dying leaves. It makes me feel like I can't nourish new life, that maybe I am just a killer, not a nurturer. Maybe things and people can't grow in my presence. Maybe I can only watch them die.

There Are Places I Remember

The poem says that April is the cruellest month, but I think it might be February. In England, February is filled with grey days and clouds. We search in vain for spots of sun on the horizon. We witness the lengthening moments of daylight, and cling desperately to the vague promise of spring.

For widows, February brings Valentine's Day, a holiday designed for couples. It slaps us in the face with the reminder that we are on our own. We try to ignore the messages and hearts all around us. We get through the day however we can. My grief group has decided to celebrate together, albeit virtually, by holding a Grief Cafe online. We'll check in with each other and remember the loves that we lost. We'll post pictures, have a laugh, and wish each other well. We'll linger in that safe place where we are understood.

The first weekend in February, four years ago, I met Stan for the first time, when I took the train from London to Manchester to visit him. I was filled with anxiety in the days before our visit, trying to shop for clothes and a coat that would add a touch of femininity to my usually androgynous appearance. I remember the excitement I felt when I stepped onto the platform and saw him waiting for me at the gate. I remember being warmed by the kindness that radiated from his spirit. It is hard to believe it was only four years ago, that I met him. I feel like I have known him all my life.

I am writing this on Saturday, and tomorrow, Sunday, is Parinirvana Day at our Centre, where we commemorate the death of the Buddha. It is a time for us to contemplate the fact of impermanence, and the preciousness of life, and to mourn those we have lost throughout the year. We will have readings and chants, and place photos of our loved ones upon the shrine. We will leave offerings of candles and incense. We will speak their names. We will remember them.

February brings all these dates that trigger memories of what I have lost--the first weekend we spent together, Valentine's Day, Parinirvana Day--but every day is a trigger for me, it seems. Each morning, I awaken with him on my heart, and each night, I ask him to come to me in my dreams, as I drift off to sleep.

In this land that belonged to him, each place in this vast landscape is also a reminder. When he first died, I could not even venture onto the High Street without being triggered by a flurry of memories—the cake shop where we chose our wedding cake, the pub where we held our reception, the jewellery shop where we bought our rings, the corner café where we ate our English breakfasts on a Sunday morning.

I can visit the shops, now, and walk through the market, without the crushing sadness and dread that I felt in those early days and weeks. I can walk into the Buddhist Centre, where a picture of him hangs on the bulletin board, and I can shake off the pain of his absence from this place he loved so much.

But I avoid most other places that he shared with me--the historic villages that wind through these hills, ancient names and places--Castleton, Bakewell, Eyam, Buxton. Century old pubs, with wooden beams and low ceilings, a log fire crackling in the middle of the room, perhaps a sheepdog or two resting in front of it, the smell of home brewed ale, the aroma of stews and soups bubbling on the stove—we'd travel miles to take in a Sunday dinner, in one of these spots.

Oh, the places he showed me! Anglesey, a beautiful village off the coast of Wales, with its tiny rutted roads, like bicycle tracks, reaching toward the sky. Bodnant Gardens, in Northern Wales, where we'd visit in April, when the rhododendrons were in bloom. Oban, in Scotland, and the isles of Staffa and Iona, in the Inner Hebrides, where we spent a glorious, sunny week, one summer, with more sun than the locals had seen in years.

There are so many more. He seemed to have an intimate connection with every inch of this land. He knew the interesting places to visit. He showed me the most stunning vistas.

And since he died, I have not been able to visit any of them. Since he died, I have been tethered to my home.

Sometimes, I feel imprisoned here, afraid to venture to the faraway places he loved best. I know I need to face my pain, and the poignant memories of our life together, in order to expand my shrunken world.

This summer, I want to make a pilgrimage, of sorts, to some of our sacred spots.

I'll head to Whitby, first, this gorgeous village on the Northeastern Coast of England, where a shell of an abbey stands, the inspiration for Bram Stoker's Dracula's castle, where rocky paths line the coastal waters, and angry waves collide with the rugged shoreline.

I'm going to hike a short distance, 25 miles, from Whitby, past Robin Hood's Bay, to Scarborough, set my feet onto the trail, my heart soothed by the ocean's rhythm. I'll camp in the grasses, among the stars. I'll pay homage to this place, where he hoped to one day retire, this place that he hoped to call home.

And I will remember him, standing at the top of the cliff, his warm eyes smiling at me, as we faced the wind, together.

Living Perpetually In Fear

I have built my entire life around the fear of loss.

I've had a string of losses, in my adult life, perhaps more than most. Each loss dug deeper wounds into my heart. Each loss wove more fear into the sorrow I felt. Each loss added layers of protection to my spirit.

I came to England in a flight from grief, after the loss of my sister and my mother, within a year of each other. Twelve months and two weeks after my mom died, we lost my sister-in-law. All the women in my family. Gone.

I lived a lonely life, here, in England, in the beginning, visiting places and travelling largely on my own, protected from the pain of relationships, isolated in a city of millions, but safe. Cocooned.

Then I met the man who would change my world.

And from the moment I fell in love with Stan, I lived in fear of losing him.

Realising I loved him filled me with excitement and joy, but that joy was tinged with an underpinning of fear. It felt like I was jumping off a great cliff.

I worried about his health. He did not have the healthiest of habits, though he was working to change his lifestyle. I used to lay my head upon his chest, when we were in bed, and listen to his heart, secretly counting the beats, checking to see if they were irregular, or too slow or too fast. If I came upon him sleeping, I would creep up next to him, and listen for his breathing.

Sometimes, he'd hold his breath, and wait until I got real close, then jump up and holler. He thought it was hilarious. "Don't be so ridiculous, BooBoo, I'm not going anywhere," he'd say.

When we went to see him at the morgue, I looked at his cold, still body on the table, and I hoped that perhaps he was just holding his breath. I hoped he'd jump up and holler, like he used to, and tell me it had all been a joke. There was no logic in these thoughts. But there is no logic in the face of such great loss.

In the aftermath, consumed with guilt over the things I had done wrong, or not done well, I thought that perhaps my constant worry, propelled into the universe, was a factor in causing his death. There are those new age gurus, out there, after all, who preach about how our thoughts create our reality, and even the Buddha said that our thoughts make the world. I wondered if it was true. I wondered if my neurosis killed him. It was not logical thinking. But logic does not figure into the shock and trauma of early grief.

I have a dear friend named Barbara, who lives in Seattle. She and I, and her sister, Nancy, were travelling buddies in our 20s, crisscrossing the country, more than once. Barb and I attended the same college, for a while, and embraced sobriety, a few months apart. The three of us remained close friends, through the years, sharing our lives in snippets, short visits, and phone calls, while living on opposite coasts. Our lives seemed to echo each other's—they lost siblings, and their mother, too. Barbara met and fell in love with someone, and married him, two months before I married Stan.

Barb's husband became ill around November of 2013, and they rode the roller coaster ride of his sickness, with ever increasing hospital visits, and brief promises of recovery, followed by further deterioration of his condition. On the 9th of April, 2014, Barbara's beloved husband died.

I grieved for her. I had never met Chris, but I knew their love was strong. I couldn't imagine the pain she must be feeling. I cried for days, thinking of her loss. It made me worry, also, about losing Stan. Life felt so tenuous and unfair. I couldn't let go of it. My fear was exacerbated, later in April, by Stan's stay in hospital for five days, with a bout of diverticulitis.

He tried to ease my fears. He told me not to worry, that he was going to be all right. He assured me that our situation was not the same as that of my friend and her husband. He held my head to his chest, and stroked my hair, as he always did, when I was afraid.

Two months later to the day, on the 9th of June, Stan was dead.

All the time I wasted, steeped in fear and worry. All the time he spent, calming my fears, convincing me that he would be okay. Precious, fleeting time. All the effort and energy expended, trying to wrestle some kind of control over life, instead of just living it—instead of just loving him.

Barbara and I speak often, to each other, now, and share this, another facet of our echoed lives. We provide a foundation of support for one another, though we live 5000 miles apart. We have lost so much of our family. We have lost our husbands. But we want to be freed from the slavery of fear, to learn to live fully these lives that are beyond our control.

We'll continue to lean upon one another. We'll help each other stay soft.

Spring

Turning Back the Clock

Stan at 10 years of age

I saw a grief post, recently, that resonated with me. It said "I wish I could turn back the clock: I'd find you sooner and love you longer."

When I read about other widows or widowers who lived with their spouses for decades, before they died, I feel sad for them. I think it must be so difficult to lose a partner with whom one has shared an entire lifetime. I think it must be very hard to learn how to be on one's own, after growing together, all those years. I feel for them.

But I must admit that underneath it all, there is a bit of envy, too. I met Stan in 2011, and he died three and a half years later. Barely enough time to settle in. They got to share young adulthood with one another, become parents, together, nurture each other through careers and middle age and perhaps even becoming grandparents. I had none of that with Stan. I only know the many parts of his life through the stories he told me, and through the memories his friends and family share with me, now that he is gone.

Stan led a colourful, varied life, with many incarnations. He never stopped changing and growing. There were people from all aspects of his life, at his funeral, from those who worked for him in the field of housing, to friends and neighbours who respected his volunteering in Glossop, to the close circle of friends that grew around bringing world music to our village, to the Buddhists who had become so close to him in recent years.

Most of those incarnations were lived before we met.

I wish I had known young Stanley, the boy, above, who excelled in scouts and had a paper route, who loved his four sisters, who cried when the snow melted into the ground. I wish I had met him when he was a teenager, riding his bicycle through the city of Manchester, picking up odd jobs, and dating pretty girls.

I wish I had known the Stan who was a young parent, taking his kids on holiday, traipsing up and down the hills of Derbyshire and the mountains in Wales, driving them down secret roads, entertaining them with his silly songs.

Or Stan, the gardener, who learned the names of all the flowers and shrubs in England, and how to nourish them, and make them grow.

Or the Stan who found reggae music, and fell in love with it, befriending the Jamaican community in their all night shebeens.

I wish I had known the fiery advocate who was a leader in the trade union movement, who organised and led a three week strike. I would have marched with him on the front lines, had I known him, then.

I used to tell him, often, that I wished we had met sooner, but he was not one to wish for things to be different than they were. He'd tell me that he was just so happy that we had found each other, when we did. He said that meeting me made him a lucky man.

I guess the Stan I knew was a combination of all those other Stans. He still remembered the names of all the flowers and shrubs. He taught me about the trade union movement, and the struggles of the working class. He shared his reggae and world music collection with me. He still drove down tiny 'secret' roads when his kids came to visit, and he still sang his silly songs.

I would have loved to witness the man he was becoming. He was delving deeper into the dharma and becoming more devoted to the Buddhist path. He had just begun to work as a part of the 'heart' team at the centre, and he was excited to use his management skills to help the centre grow. He was improving his diet, looking after himself, letting go of past indulgences, changing his life, yet again.

I like to think I had a little to do with his newfound transformation. I like to think that my love and support helped him to grow and blossom into the man he wanted to be.

I know that his love helped me grow. He helped me open to others. He helped me learn to be comfortable in my own skin. He taught me to treat myself with a gentle touch.

Meeting him made me a lucky woman.

I didn't get to share decades with my husband. I didn't get to know him in his youth, or grow with him through young adulthood and middle age. We didn't get to grow old together. But we shared a lifetime in our few short years.

Tender Touch

I awakened last night, and reached for my husband in the dark, only to find that now familiar, empty space, instead. And I remembered how I would drape my leg over his, at night, and press my stomach against his back. Sometimes, he would stir, slightly, and tell me to take my leg off of him. He said my legs were too heavy. He referred to them as tree trunks. And I'd tell him that his legs were like twigs.

When we first met, he delighted in my body, and I, in his. We knew each other so well, every curve and spot. We were not young, and we sagged and puffed with age, a bit, but that didn't seem to matter, much. We fit together. He used to tell me that he loved my body. No one had ever said that to me, or made me believe it.

There is something so beautiful about sharing intimate touch. There is no replacement for it. Hugs from friends help, but it is not the same. It is bigger than sex. It is being seen, and felt, and known, and accepted—every part. It is the intertwining of two worlds. It is knowing each other's rhythms and ways. It is a softening, a melding. It is the weaving of two lives into one.

At night, we would lie next to each other, in our bed, and talk. We'd share painful memories, our fears and worries. We'd resolve conflicts, settle differences, say the things that might be too hard to express in the light of day. He'd hear me crying, reach for my cheek, brush the tears away with his soft fingertips. He'd pull me close and stroke my hair.

These are the moments I ache for.

These are the times that feel most desolate: when I awaken in the night, and find him missing; in the morning, when I rise, without the sound of his breathing next to me—the room silent, and bereft.

I fill these restless moments, that stretch into late night hours, with information and internet. On the worst nights, I watch murder mysteries on the telly. On better nights, I listen to a dharma talk. But always I must drown the quiet, and chase away the memories. The emptiness and silence are just too much to bear.

The night before he died, Stan lay upon the sofa, and I sat next to him, pulled his legs onto my lap, and rubbed his aching calves. His calves were always hard, and painful to the touch. I stroked them softly, as we watched silly shows on TV. His youngest son was here with us. Stan was quiet and pensive, as if in a bubble of his own.

I crept up the stairs, before him, and when he came to bed, he turned his back to me, and I let him be. His son had died two weeks before, and we were headed to the funeral the following day. I didn't know how to reach my husband. I thought he wanted space.

Oh! How I wish I had wrapped my arms around him, and pressed myself into his back. How I wish I had whispered in his ear that I would be there for him, no matter what, that we would get through this together, that I would be, always, at his side.

But I didn't. I kissed his cheek, told him goodnight, and turned my back to his.

In the morning, I brought him his tea. I scrubbed his back, in the bath, laid out his funeral suit, wiped the dust from his good shoes. I helped him dress. Straightened his tie.

I held his hand at the funeral, and put my arm around his shoulder, after he had read the tribute to his son.

I held his hand tightly in mine as we walked out the door of the chapel. Felt it slip from my grasp as he crumbled to the ground.

The 9th of June, 2014. Exactly nine months ago, today.

Our final, tender touch.

Ashes to Ashes

Saturday, I carried the remnants of my husband's body from our bedroom to the summit of Monks Road, in Glossop, the spot he had chosen as his final resting place. It was one of the hardest things I have had to do, in this 10 month journey since his death.

His family and I scheduled this date months ago. Even then, I was reluctant to consider it. It was a comfort to me, to have his scatter tube here, in our room, underneath the photo of us, taken at our wedding. I loved the little shrine I had made for him. I would touch and pat the tube as I talked to him. I would say hello to him in the morning and tell him good night when I came upstairs for bed.

To those who have not yet faced the loss of a spouse, (or, perhaps, even, to some who have), this might seem a bit creepy. But it felt no different than visiting a beloved's grave. I knew where he was, and I felt grounded by his presence.

This act of cremation, so popular in recent years, feels unsettling to me. I understand the need for it, and perhaps it is more ecologically sound, but, had it been my choice, I think I would have preferred our traditional custom of burial. It feels so much more concrete. We place our loved ones in the ground, and shovel dirt on top. We memorialise them with a stone. We etch their names into it, and their dates of birth and death. We go to their graves and place flowers, and trinkets, touch the ground where their body rests. Their lives are made permanent, somehow, through these rituals.

In cremation, we reduce their bodies to a bucket of ash. We scatter them to the winds. They are lost to us, forever.

It feels so final.

I know that he was so much more than his body. His spirit was bigger than that. I know that he lives on in our memories and in our hearts. I hope that my written words will serve as a concrete reminder of who he was and what he meant to all of us. Still, it was hard to say goodbye to what little I had left.

Saturday came, and the date had arrived, and it was time to carry out his wishes. His children, especially, felt the need to have a place to visit, too. It was selfish of me to keep him hidden away, inside a room, when he had always made clear his desire to become a part of that sloping hill at the top of our world, where, on a clear day, the view stretches more than twenty miles, to the cities below.

I brought his ashes down the stairs and placed them in a carrier bag. I wrapped them in a blanket so they wouldn't be cold, and I seat belted him into the car to bring them to his son's house. The morning was damp and grey, and predictions ranged from drizzle to hard rain, typical weather for northern England, in the spring.

I asked him to clear the way for us to do what we needed to do for him. I could hear him saying "it's the weather! Just deal with it!" Or, his famous line--"the leaves are dancing in the rain! You should be dancing, too!"

The family and I gathered at his son's house, before heading to the summit—the house where we had gathered on the 9th of June, to form a caravan behind the hearse that carried another son's casket—the same place we gathered, two weeks later, to follow his casket.

Thirty minutes before we made our pilgrimage to the hill, the weather cleared, and the rains paused. We drove a mile to the summit, where his good friends and sisters waited. We brought his scatter tube to a flat place, and I read parts from a poem he had written, in 2010, shortly before we met.

From **"The Buddleia and Two Butterflies"**
By Stan Kukalowicz, September 2010

Oh the sheer beauty of the Buddleia, emerging from barren ground,
With pinnacles of vivid navy blue, cheekily inviting you to come and view.

Butterflies descend, performing a rhythmic dance amongst the hues,
Each splendid in their beauty and vibrancies, inviting you to taste.

Previous experiences now pupated into a delicate and colourful creation.

We passed his tube, from me, to daughters, to sons, to sisters, each of us scattering a piece of him to the ground. We threw flowers amongst the ashes as offerings. We hugged each other and wiped our tears. We piled back into cars and made our way down the hill. And the rains resumed.

I had dreaded this day for months. I had tried to ignore its looming closeness. I had not wanted to let him go. But the next morning, I awakened with a sense of calm, and relief. We had honoured his wishes. We had placed the remnants of the body we loved into the earth, where the winds would carry them, and the rains would wet them, and the mud would welcome them. It was hard for all of us, but we did it. He would have been proud.

I have taken the day off from work today, and I am going to go for a little hike, up the hill, to his spot. I'll take a flower, and say hello.

Later in the spring, we'll plant a bush—a buddleia—a hearty plant, wild, and beautiful, where butterflies like to rest.

By the Sea, On My Own

The Village of Whitby

It is a glorious spring day on the northern coast of England, and I am seated on a bench overlooking the sea, in a village called Robin Hood's Bay. It is an ancient settlement, with remains found that date back 3000 years, and first mentioned by a topographer of Henry the VIII in 1536.

Yesterday I walked to this village from Whitby, where I am staying, this weekend, on the first part of my pilgrimage to visit the places Stan and I loved. Of all of them, the village of

Whitby, and this northern coast, were his favourite. He often spoke of retiring here, where he said they had 'proper winters.'

All around me families stroll along the shore, children running happily toward the waves with their plastic shovels and buckets filled with sand. Couples walk hand in hand, deep in conversation or silent in contemplation. Dogs of all sizes frolic along the water, chasing balls and rings thrown by their owners into the sea. The water must be freezing, but no one seems to mind. The English have stripped down to shorts and tank tops and let the waves curl around their bare feet. It is the first real warmth we have had all year. We have been so desperate for the sun.

It has been a gorgeous weekend. I have walked to the places he loved best. I have ambled along the grounds of Whitby Abbey, a monastery that once held a community of Benedictine nuns and monks, set high above the village, at the top of a hill, said to be the inspiration for Bram Stoker's "Dracula's Castle". I have visited the seaside museum, in Robin Hood's Bay, where Stan and I read the exhibits and played the games like little kids. I have visited the independent book store, where he waited patiently outside, while I got lost in there, pouring through the collections of plays and poetry and children's books.

My time here has been peaceful, and solitary, walking for miles along the cliffs that hug the shoreline, and climbing amongst the slippery rocks while the tide was out. I like to think he has been here with me, walking alongside me, sharing my steps. Stan had problems with mobility, so he couldn't walk far, and hiking was not a love I could share with him. But he would try to go as far as he could, then he would find a bench to sit and watch the world, while I walked for an hour or two without him. When I'd return, he'd be sitting, happily, in the same place, observing, listening, being. He was the most patient person I have ever known.

On Saturday, I walked from the trail down to the seaside, and climbed around on some slippery rocks, trying to get closer to the waves. With one unmindful moment, I fell, hard, against them, almost smashing my face, and possibly breaking my thumb. It was an isolated cove, with few other people, and I realised that, had I broken a leg or something, it would be hours, probably, before anyone would find me. And, I thought, what if no one finds me? There was no phone service, there. And no one knew where I was. Eventually, someone in Stan's family might become concerned and send a search party, perhaps a day or two past my planned return. But by then I might have perished.

And, if I do break a leg, or an arm, or a hip, as women my age are prone to do, in a fall, I thought, who would look after me? I am not one to ask for help.

The next day, stepping amongst the rocks at the seaside, I was much more cautious, and afraid to take risks. I can't afford to get hurt. It made me feel the full depth of this being alone.

There are so many things I miss about sharing a life with my beloved husband, but, of all of them, it is the sense of having someone look out for me that I miss most. There is no one to do that, now. I know there are people who care, but it is not the same as having a person. Folks who have lost their spouses will understand. It is the feeling that there is someone who has your back--that there is one person in the world who cares if you are hurt, or sad, or feeling poorly. It is the safety in knowing that your person will be there, when something goes wrong, to help you through it, to ease your suffering. It is the security of knowing that you do not have to traverse this often difficult path of life on your own.

For a few, short years, I had a brief respite, when I was a part of something bigger, when I had someone to share the burden, when I knew that someone had my back. But he is gone, and I am, once again, on my own, forced to rely on my own resources. I have been taking care of myself since I was very young, and today, it makes me feel so tired.

I climb the path to the top of the hill, overlooking the sea, to take the bus back to Whitby. And I remember the day we climbed this hill together. I was so excited to get to the top, so that I could take a photo, to capture the beauty of this place, but the climb was very hard for Stan, and he had to pause, often, to rest his legs. He'd sit on one of the many benches they provide, and ask me to join him, and I would, though I could barely hide my desire to make it to the top. His mobility issues made him able to pause, more often, to move through life more slowly, more mindfully, to see the world around him, to watch, and listen, and be. He didn't have to take photos to capture beauty. He was able to be a part of it, as it happened.

Tomorrow, I will make my way back home, to our stone cottage, in the middle of our own little paradise. The predictions are for a few days of sun and temperatures rising to 70 degrees Fahrenheit--a heat wave, here in England. I'll try to remember to pause, and take it in. I'll try to feel for his presence, around me, looking after me, from wherever he is, to let his memory wash over me, and help me to feel less alone.

To Everything, There is a Season

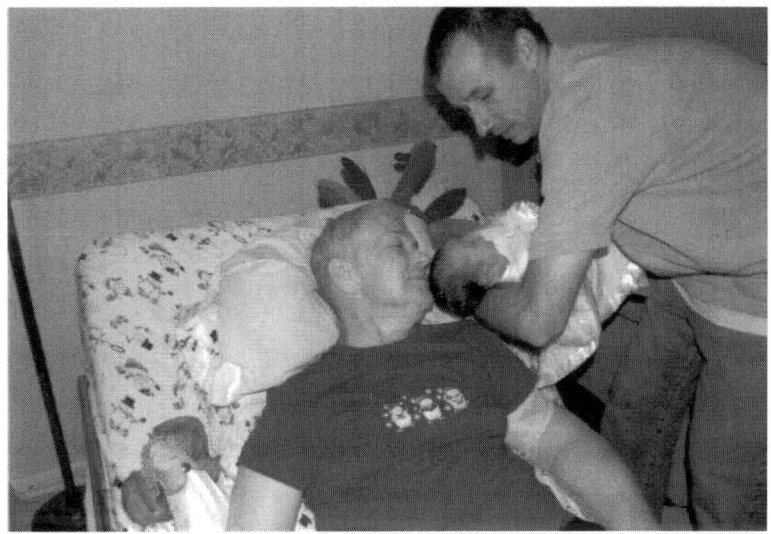

My sister, Debra, shortly before her death, meeting her newborn niece

Spring has sprung in Northern England, and everywhere life is blooming. Magnolia trees burst with pink and white flowers, their sweet scent wafting along with the evening winds. Baby lambs, their legs still wobbly, hover near their mothers' stomachs, with tender young faces that seem to be smiling. Birdsong fills the air, the cacophony so loud at first light that, often, it startles me awake. The sun warms dark black dirt in the allotments nearby, as gardeners turn the earth with their shovels and hoes to prepare it for planting. Our spirits are uplifted, our hearts filled with hope that, perhaps, the long winter is behind us.

My husband loved this transition from winter into spring. As much as he cautioned me to accept and rejoice in the weather, whatever it bestowed upon us, the sun's bright rays and the increasing hours of daylight brought a lightness to his step. He'd open the curtains in the mornings, and do his little dance, as the sun shone through our bedroom window. He'd take us for long drives among the hills, pointing out and naming the flowers along the roadside. He'd take me lilac hunting through the village, showing me all the gardens that held the bushes of my favourite flowers in bloom. We'd drive to Miller's Dale, where there was a flat trail that was easy for him to navigate, pausing our walk to stand by the pond and watch the ducks and the Canada geese as they paddled through its waters.

Life unfolds all around me, but I live, also, in the shadow of death.

We are taught that to everything, there is a season. There are poems and bible verses and dharma teachings and even songs written about it. But most of us choose to ignore what looms so closely. We want to revel in the spring. We carry on as if the autumn will never reach us. We don't want to acknowledge the season of death.

It is different for those of us who have faced great loss. We know it is ever present. We know that there is a thin, delicate veil between life and death. We have seen it. We have watched life slip from our loved ones, and death overtake them. It has happened before our very eyes. We can't turn back, dancing only in the joy of spring. We have seen and felt the dark days of death's winter.

The photo above was taken at Thanksgiving, 2007, three weeks before my sister passed. She was too weak to go anywhere, so the family gathered around her, at my house, where she slept, most of the day, in the hospital bed I had set up for her. Our niece, Alberta, had just given birth to her first child, and her husband brought the baby close to my sister, so she could take in the smell of newborn life.

The photo is such a poignant reminder, for me, of the juxtaposition of life and death--my sister Debra, leaving this world, just as my great-niece, Lily, enters it.

Last year, at this time, I, too, stood in the juxtaposition between life and death, and somehow, a part of me must have known it. My good friend, Barbara, had just said goodbye to her husband, who died of liver failure, too sick to benefit from the donor one they had procured for him. I learned how she had to tell her husband that there was no hope, then had to witness his deterioration, and, finally, to turn off his life support.

Though I did not know Chris, Barb and I had been friends for over 30 years, and her loss was devastating to me. I couldn't imagine how she summoned the strength and the courage to weather this tragedy. I grieved for her, and I began to obsess about the possibility of losing Stan. The trajectory of life had often been similar for my friend and me. I was frightened that maybe this was an omen.

My friends, and Stan, himself, tried to allay my worries. They soothed me with kind words and told me that it was only my fear of loss that was at play. They assured me that such a terrible event could not happen twice.

Last April, our mild winter easily gave way to the new life of spring, and the warmth in the air was palpable. Stan had just begun a new position at the Manchester Buddhist Centre, and he was excited about its prospects. But he was feeling tired and worn out, and his stomach was bothering him, with sometimes excruciating pains. After a sleepless night of increasing discomfort, I drove him to the GP, and he ended up in hospital. Diverticulitis, they said, with a large abscess that had spread infection through his body. He was placed on IV antibiotics for 5 days, and sent home with another 5 day round of them.

He was slowly recovering, by the 1st of May, so I carried on with my plans to go to New York to visit my son. I saw my friend Barbara, there, and sat with her in her grief. Still, I worried about losing Stan. But others assured me he was on the mend. I had to remind myself that this tragedy of my friend's was not about me.

When I returned to England, Stan was distant. He said he was not feeling himself. There was nothing particular that he could point to, to describe it. He said he just felt tired. We figured it was part of the long path of recovery from his recent illness. Then his son was found dead, and our focus turned toward making funeral plans while swimming through our shock and grief. Two weeks later, Stan was gone. That thin veil between life and death was lifted, once again.

After we drove to my home, having left his body at the hospital, I stood at the stone fence overlooking my beloved hills. It was summer, and the heat cast a swirl of haze over the village. I rested my body against the cool stone, and phoned my son and his girlfriend. They are not usually so easily available by phone, and had just emerged from a 7 day, silent retreat, but they answered. And they were on the next plane from New York to meet me in my sorrow.

As the first anniversary of my husband's death draws near, I replay this sequence of events in my head, and on the page, over and over. It feels important to me to remember it. I write to put into words all the confusion and clutter that lives inside me, to untangle the twisted and knotted threads of this complicated grief.

I have been visited by the spectre of death. It is a visitor that refuses to leave me. My intimate connection with this unwanted guest has changed me forever. I hope that, somewhere, beyond the immediacy of this grief, my understanding of the thin veil between life and death has made me kinder. I hope it has made me more patient. I hope it has helped me to recognise what truly matters, in this short life, and to put aside the petty irritations and quarrels that cause so much suffering.

I will live, always, with the shadow of death. I hope it helps me to savour the sunlight.

Reach Deep, Find Warmth

I have been nestled inside the winter for months, it seems. It has been so cold and dark. Even today, at the end of April, spring struggles to gain a grip, the wind and rain overtaking its warm and promising breezes, painting the hilltops white, again, pouring pellets of icy hail onto the ground. This weekend, there are predictions of frost.

Each day, I walk past the newly budding lilacs on my way to the train station, and I kiss them, and tell them to be strong, and reach deep, and find warmth. I so hope the cold will not kill them before they flower.

I have sat inside an inner winter, too. Some days, I am able to look around, and revel in the rainbow coloured tulips and the deep blues and violets of the evening sky. But other days, I cannot reach deep enough to overcome the cold, and the world feels frozen, the wind biting at my fingertips.
I am writing this post a few days early, as, on Friday, I am travelling to Spain, to spend a week on a farm animal sanctuary called Pig Village, where I will bask in the sun, and rub pigs' bellies, and feed the chickens and donkeys that roam the fields, there, free to live out their lives without fear of slaughter. My heart needs me to be with animals, to work, and to sweat. Perhaps I can store the heat in my bones to keep me warm through the unsettled days of this English spring.

I am treading slowly toward the anniversary of my husband's death. Last night I remembered how I left him, on the 2nd of May, at the Manchester Airport, to come to the US to visit my son. I left him. I went off to New York, to watch my son graduate from University, to see his final, solo performance, to visit friends and hike gorges and savour the beauty of the waterfalls. All the while, my husband was here, in England, on his own.

17 days, we were apart. We spoke on FaceTime, but I was distracted. I knew we would be together very soon. I was in my own little world. It was the price he paid, I told myself, for marrying an ex-pat. I needed to visit folks in America, and we could not afford for both of us to travel there, each year. We'd work out ways to minimise this stress, I thought. We'd discuss it upon my return.

Three weeks after I came back to my husband, he was dead.

How could I do it? How could I have left him, alone? Why didn't I pay more attention to him, when we spoke? How could I not somehow know that we were in the countdown of his life?And how do I learn to forgive myself for something I could not possibly have predicted? How long will I pour over the details of our last days together, wishing it had been other than it was? When will I see that I can't change what happened? How do I let this go?

Oh. It is so easy to crawl back into the depths of winter. The colours of my life were just beginning to emerge. Not brilliant colours, not bright. No fiery reds and oranges with their passion for living. Just soft and flowing pastel hues. But colour, nonetheless. Light and hope against the darkness.

Yet, the weather has turned cold, again. I feel a freeze coming. My purple lilac buds might not make it. My colours may just fade away, carried along on the wind of these memories.

Be strong, I must tell myself. Reach deep. Find warmth.

Summer

Nero's Cry

This week, on an animal sanctuary in Southern Spain, I am surrounded by rock, and the nude, bare earth echoes the inner emptiness I feel. In England, all that green and growing doesn't match my insides. Here, this rock, this heat, this rugged blend of pine and desert wildflower, poking up from parched earth, speaks to my spirit. Here, amongst this rock, my heart feels at ease.

I awaken at early light and walk the dirt path to the pig run, and enter their space. Carmella comes to smell and nudge me with her snout, and I place my hand upon her coarse, bristled skin. I sit in the dirt and wait for her to realise that I will not hurt her, and, after a few moments, she lies down next to me. I stretch my legs around her so that I can rub her belly, and she rolls on her side so that I can get a better reach. She grunts her pleasure and closes her eyes. I breathe deep. I slow my breathing to match hers, in rhythm and depth, and I rub her until she's had enough, awakens from her brief slumber, and rises, moving on toward the back of the pen. Our encounter is a healing balm for us both.

In the morning hours, we stroke and feed and water the animals, or work in the garden. My skin bakes in the sun, from pasty white to the brown shade of rock that encircles this vast landscape. Here, my ears have a rest from the noise of city life. Here, I listen to the call of the birds, the neighing of horses, the barking of dogs, the grunting of pigs.

In the early afternoon, as the sun beats down hard upon the earth, we are summoned inside, to the cool of the dining room, where our generous host nourishes us with healthy and delicious vegan dishes. I gather with the other volunteers around the welcoming wooden table, and we eat and laugh and rest, together, with this family that has opened itself to strangers, and made us all friends.

They asked me to write down my next of kin as an emergency contact. Next of kin? My next of kin are all gone. Not really. I do have family. But they are far away, in America, and wouldn't be of much help, should something happen to me, here.

I am an orphan. Most of my family has passed before me. I have piled their deaths, one by one, like a pile of rocks, stretching up to this clear, clean, immense, blue sky. My father, my sister, my mother, and now. The love of my life, swept away from me in an instant, after it took me decades to find him.

I am awash in death.

I have friends in England. I have Stan's family, and I know they would be there for me. But I was only a part of their lives for a few years before Stan died. I wonder what they thought of me when I first came around. Perhaps they saw me as just another of his tenuous relationships, one of many he had had in his recent life, in his quest to find the one who understood him and loved him without condition. I like to think that I was that one. I like to think that he was able to settle in, a bit, when he met me, and realise that he had someone who would care for him and nurture his growth and spirit. I hope his children recognised the love and affection that passed between us. I hope they know how much he meant to me.

But next of kin?
My next of kin is dead. Gone with the wind.

These are the thoughts I have, as I sit here, my body warmed by the scorching heat. In this space, among these kind people, I have found a bit of reprieve from the relentless grief. In this vast, wild landscape, I unfurl my sorrow, and let it rest.

At night, I walk to my tent by the light of the full moon, to the song of the doves and nightingales. Some folks are bothered by their loud singing, and must close the flaps of their tents and plug their ears in order to sleep. But I keep the tent flaps open, shielded only by the screen. In the distance, the village church bells ring their signal every hour, on the hour. I count them.

Twelve. It is midnight. The clanging bells are my only anchor to the time, here. I drift off to sleep with the sounds of the earth all around me.

There is a donkey here, named Nero. He is very social. He holds his head over the low fence so that I can stroke his forehead and ears. He loves to be touched. When I walk away from him, his bottom lip quivers, and he lets out a boisterous bray that echoes off these rugged rocks.

Every night, around three a.m., Nero awakens the world with his mournful wail. He calls out with all the strength he can muster. I'm alone, he says. He raises his brown face toward the moon. His cry is loud enough to startle the deepest sleepers. I'm alone. I'm alone. Come visit.

I find comfort in this donkey's wail. I love to hear it in the night. If I had the courage, I would rise, unzip the screen of my tent, and rush to his side. I would raise my face to the moon, open my vocal chords, and meet his wail with my own. I'd call out loud enough so that all those who have passed before me could hear it. My father. My sister. My mother. My love.

I'm alone. I'm alone. Come visit.

Life Piles Up

Me, Stan, and Gavin

It is the middle of May, now, and we are moving toward the anniversary of your death. Sunday, May 24th, is the day the police came to tell us they had found your son, dead, in his flat. I remember that moment as if it happened yesterday. It was a Saturday afternoon, and we had not long returned from our weekly shop. We were relaxing on the sofa, and watching a silly show. You put the show on pause to answer the doorbell. Our doorbell was set to the melody of "It's a Small World," an apt tune, for us.

I remember your face when you walked through the door, with the police officers trailing behind you. All the colour had drained out of it. They sat on one sofa, while we sat on the other. They asked you to tell them about Gavin. I remember you talked about him for a long time, about his struggles in his life, how he had been doing so much better, in the past year, but how it seemed that, recently, his life had again taken a downward turn. Perhaps you were trying to stave off the inevitable. Then the words came: "Well, sir, there is no easy way to say this, but..."

I remember how your face fell. You took off your glasses, and the tears came, and you brushed them quickly away. The officers lingered for a few moments, while we poured over the details: where he was found, what they knew, which was nothing, where to find his body, now, and when it could be released. I still have the card, in the drawer of the coffee table, that the kind officer gave us, with his name and contact details. Officer Leigh Carnally. He put his hand upon your shoulder, as they stood and said goodbye. "I'm so sorry for your loss."

I sat beside you. We were both in shock. I had thought that perhaps they had come to tell us Gavin was in trouble, but you said no, the police here don't come round for that. You knew, the moment you opened the door, what they had come to tell you. You had been dreading this day for twenty years.

Life has piled up without you. It is hard to recall all the things that have happened since that day, and the day, two and a half weeks later, of your death. I remember every detail of those days and weeks. But since then? It has been a blur. I have put one foot in front of the other, and I have swum through this cesspool of grief. I don't know how I have done it. I have managed to get to the shops, to purchase vegetables and bread. I have mopped the floors, hoovered the carpets, met with solicitors, changed the mortgage, conferred with creditors, paid the bills. I have taken care of all the little things I used to detest, the things you used to take care of, for us, when you were here.

Meanwhile I have carried your memory around in my arms, like a basket of fruit, doling out pieces of you to anyone who cared to listen. I like to tell people about your ways. I like to reflect on how you were able to be present, with life, and how, in spite of all your childhood strife, and previous struggles, you were so content. I like to share funny stories about your eccentricities and quirks. It makes me feel closer to you, somehow.

Your grandchildren have flourished, this year. One of them has passed her driver's test, on the first try, not an easy feat, here in England. She thought of you when she passed it. She knew you would be so proud of her. She and her cousin, your other grandchild, have been accepted at University, and will be going there, in the autumn. Your other grandson has grown, in inches and in maturity. Remember how you used to put him on your lap? It would not be so easy to do that, now.

Your children miss you. There have been rivers of tears shed, for you and for Gavin, this year. They have tried to carry on without you, and to live in a way that would make you proud. They are such kind and compassionate and loving people, your kids. You raised them well.

Me? I, too, have tried to live this life without you, this life I did not choose, in a way that would make you proud. I have had many wobbles along the way. I have had days where all I could do was curl up under the duvet and watch mindless telly. I have had days where I couldn't leave the house, because my face has been puffed and swollen and blotched with tears. But always I manage to move through it. I get up the next day and go out into the world. I read, I write, I hike, I meditate, I am even doing a bit of yoga, most days.

Your beloved Sangha is now a big part of my life. They have welcomed me with their open, loving arms. This weekend, we are gathering down south, for a Sangha retreat. There will be about seventy of us, there. I know you'll be there, too. You will linger in the hearts and minds of those who loved you. We'll share memories and have a laugh.

It has been almost a year since you left us, and life has piled up without you. I don't know how it happened. I don't know what to do with the time I have left. I wish you were here to guide me, with your gentle wisdom and support. I've had to let go of your physical presence. I miss your embrace, your warmth, your touch.

But as long as I walk this planet, your spirit will live. I'll carry my basket of memories in my arms, and share parts of you with everyone I meet. I'll try to live in a way that will honour you. I'll step into this life I did not choose, and one day, perhaps, I will be able to embrace it. I know you would want that for me. I know you would want me to live.

This, Too, Shall Pass

When my husband and I were 'new', and so full of love for each other, he would caution me that this aspect of our relationship, the euphoria and the intensity, would change. "It won't always feel like this," he would say. Extremist that I am, my heart opened and softened by his attentiveness, I did not believe it for a moment. I had found, finally, the love of my life, I thought, and the boundless love I felt for him would remain, and express itself, always, in exactly this way.

But, as with so many things, Stan was right. Our relationship shifted. We became more comfortable with each other, and able to focus on other parts of our lives. We grew to understand each other's rhythms and ways. We learned each other's triggers and soft spots. We shared past and present joys and sorrows. We learned how to live life, not gazing, constantly, into each other's eyes, but hand in hand, and facing the world. Together. Our relationship changed. It deepened. It grew, and developed, and got better, with the passage of time.

We didn't have enough time together. Only three and a half years. I so wanted to grow old with him by my side, to enrich our relationship as we aged. As the first anniversary of his death nears, I grieve, not only for him, but for us, and for all that we could have been.

This, too, shall pass. He would say that to me, often, in many different ways. He had a wisdom and a knowing that came from somewhere beyond this mundane existence. His wisdom came, not only from years of practise and formal study, although he did that, too. It came from his life experience, his willingness to be open to what that experience had to teach him, his ability to dig deep, and reflect. I appreciated all those aspects of him, when he was alive. But I see them more clearly, now, as I come to know him in a different light.

Our relationships with our loved ones continue to shift and to grow, even after their deaths.

As my relationship with him changes, and I integrate him into the new life I am taking on, my relationship with the house that we shared has also begun to shift. When he first died, I was adamant that I would remain here, where he was, where we were, together, forever. I made all the arrangements to assume the mortgage, as a widow, as the house was only in his name, when he died. I couldn't imagine living anywhere else. I wanted to be surrounded by his things, in the midst of his community, comforted by his spirit.

But recently, I have begun to notice a shift in my feelings. It is difficult for me, sometimes, to live where he was, where we were, together. It is so painful. I see him walking down the steps, one at a time, in the evenings, after his bath. When I come in from work, I still want to call for him, and tell him I'm home. I remember sitting with him, on this sofa, the last night of his life. I am immersed in him, every moment, when I am in this house. Sometimes I use the noise of the television and the distraction of internet to escape the constant onslaught of memories. Sometimes it is just too much. And all that distraction is not healthy for me, either. Sometimes I feel imprisoned by this place.

Yet the thought of letting go of it is also excruciatingly painful. What if I move somewhere else, and I lose him? What if I can't find him anymore? I tear up just thinking about it.

This weekend, I gathered with my sangha at a retreat centre south of here. It was a beautiful setting, and the sun warmed my face as I walked amongst the fields of buttercups and dandelions. Away from the home we shared, freed, for a moment, from the visions and memories, I felt a sense of peace.

He was present, too, at the retreat, with all of our sangha friends. We remembered him, and collected money for the fund set up in his name. People gave generously in tribute to him, and to carry on the work that he had begun to implement, at our centre. I felt his presence among us, and I knew that, had he been alive, we would have attended this retreat, together. But the memories were not so overwhelming, and constant. I was able to breathe, and relax, and reflect on how I am to carry on, in this life, on my own. And I began to consider the possibility of selling this house.

Yet, when I arrived home, I felt, too, a sense of comfort and peace. I was happy to be back. I made myself a warm drink and thought of him. I tidied up, and talked to him, as I often do, at night. Then I went to bed. Our bed.

I don't know, yet, what the future holds. I know that, if I am to stay here, I need to make some changes, and make it my own. It has been left virtually untouched since the morning we left here, together, for Gavin's funeral. I haven't had the heart to alter it.

I am not going to make any rash decisions. There is so much to consider. But it feels good to be open to the possibility of change, to not hold hard and fast to my earlier, rigid stance. I am changing. My relationship with him, and with our house, is changing.

All things change. And this, too, shall pass.

As Memories Fade

Today is the first day of June, and eight days from the first anniversary of my beloved husband's sudden death. While last year, at this time, England was sweltering under a heat wave, the temperature has barely climbed above 55F (13C) this spring. I check the weather forecast obsessively, grasping for some sign of a sliver of warmth. I want to lie in a field of grass and let the sun shed light on the dark and frozen places inside me. I want to warm the parts that are numb.

It's been almost a year since he was here with me, and sometimes that feels so long ago. I don't want to lose the memories I have. I don't want them to fade with the passage of time. But lately, I have felt him slipping from my grasp.

I remember his unique turns of phrases, his funny sayings, his mispronounced words. I remember his crooked smile, the right side of his lips slightly higher than the left. I remember how he laughed nervously when he was embarrassed, and how he rubbed his forehead with his right hand when he was upset. I remember his little dance, each forefinger in the air, when he was happy, and how his body leapt with joy and excitement when he'd see a rabbit on the hillside.

I can't remember the sound of his voice. But part of me is afraid to hear it.

I have a DVD, here, of our wedding ceremony, but I have not been able to watch it. I am afraid that seeing him on video, and hearing him speak, would be too much. I can't imagine listening to the songs we played, during the ceremony—"Is This Love," by Bob Marley, (his choice), and "In My Life" by the Beatles (mine). I don't know what seeing our first kiss as husband and wife would do to me.

I'm glad I have the video. But I have no idea when it will feel safe enough for me to watch it.

There are so many memories that I am afraid to revisit. I have clambered out of a deep, dark, hole, in the last year. I feel myself barely teetering on a precipice, and I am afraid to upset this tenuous balance. I have to be mindful of which memories my heart can absorb. One careless move could break it apart.

Every night, when I lie in bed, I ask Stan to come to me in my dreams, and last night, he was there. I was sitting in the back seat of a car, and I saw him standing with someone else, on the sidewalk, resting his hands upon a walking stick. He was wearing a pair of hideous polyester trousers that were pulled up high above his waist. I remember thinking he never wore his pants like that, and he certainly never wore polyester. I thought I was going to have to buy him some new ones, as soon as I could.

He saw me, and a broad smile crossed his face. He dropped his walking stick, danced his dance, and rushed to open the car door. He flew into the back seat and laid his head upon my chest. We were so happy to be in each other's arms again. I kissed and rubbed the top of his bald head, and I felt so full and alive.

Then I woke up.

I have carried that dream with me all day—the feel of his head, his weight pressed against me. How he nuzzled into my arms, and how I rubbed his face lightly with my fingertips. How happy we were to be with each other. How we realised, in that moment, what a treasure we had.

On this first anniversary of my husband's death, I'll hold tight to this memory of him in my dreams—his dance, his smile, his head pressed against my chest—our love, so solid and strong.

It is a memory I am not afraid to revisit. It is a memory I'll let linger, still.

It is what I have left of the man I loved—these memories of a life we shared.

Making It To The Top

Tomorrow, the day after this posting, marks the first anniversary of my beloved husband's death. I can hardly believe it is true. One year.

It feels like yesterday. It feels like a lifetime ago.

So much has changed since he died. I have done many things, in spite of my crushing grief. I have visited my home neighbourhood in Indiana, and sat with pigs and donkeys on an animal sanctuary in Spain. I have travelled to Whitby in Yorkshire and to Ireland and to Snowdonia in Wales. I have spent days and weeks in meditation, study, and reflection with my sangha teachers and friends. I have helped form a grief support group with a widowed friend in Sheffield. I have written for this blog.

And some days, I have not been able to pull myself up from the grief. I have stayed on the sofa with the curtains closed. I have slept for hours throughout the day and into the night. I have had periods of insomnia where I could not sleep more than an hour or two at a time.

Such has been the landscape of my grief. Activity and exhaustion. Periods of joy and hope followed by deep sadness. Despair and loneliness and friendship and gratitude and love.

A few months ago, I decided to mark this anniversary by doing something big, to honour my husband, and to raise money for a fund at the Buddhist Centre that was set up in his name.

Stan believed strongly that the teachings of Buddhism, the Dharma, should be accessible to everyone. It always bothered him that our retreats were too expensive for working class folks to attend them. We have beautiful retreat centres, in the UK, and our retreats are a time of study, reflection, meditation, building friendship, and renewal. They help us reconnect with what is important and to learn more of what the Buddha taught. He wanted to set up a fund to help people who couldn't afford it attend these retreats. When he died, the Buddhist Centre used the donations people made in his memory to set up this fund, and they named it the Stan Kukalowicz Bursary fund.

So I decided to hike to the top of a mountain, and get sponsors for my hike, to replenish this fund. Initially, I planned to do this on my own. It never occurred to me to ask people to commit to do it with me. But when I mentioned it to my study group, several of them offered to join me on the hike. We set up a donation page and publicised our walk.

Mount Snowdon, in Snowdonia, is the highest peak in England and Wales. At 3560 feet, it is subject to unpredictable weather, winds, and torrential rains, and its peak is most often hidden in mist and cloud. There are six paths to the summit, and I chose the second easiest one, the Snowdon Ranger Path.

In the weeks leading up to this hike, I found myself wondering what on earth I was thinking when I committed to such a feat. This peak may not seem high, in American terms, but the ascent was steep, and the conditions could be tough, and I had not disciplined myself to training regularly for it, beyond a few day hikes in the moors and regularly using the stairs to my fourth floor office at work. How was I going to do this, I wondered, if the sadness of the anniversary overtook me? Why did I not make space for myself to feel the sadness, and sit with it? What possessed me to plan such a physically strenuous event? After I had advertised my plans to everyone I knew, and with donations trickling, and then pouring in, I could not exactly cancel it, either.

I spent days obsessively checking and trying to predict the weather. Initial forecasts showed a breezy but dry day with good visibility. My friends and I were hopeful that the weather would be kind to us.

We began our journey at 10 a.m. Two hours in, and half way up the trail, the weather took a turn. Clouds began to form at the top of the peak, and winds swirled around us. We struggled to climb the switchback rocky trail as the winds gusted up to 40 miles per hour. Wiser people might have turned back. But we had committed to get to the summit, and we wanted to take a photo, when we got there.

Along the way, a seagull hovered near us. He followed us as we walked. In our brief moments of rest, he'd perch upon a rock near our stops.

On a journey that would normally take a couple of hours, we were still climbing the mountain, at four. We put one foot in front of the other and braced ourselves against the biting winds. My sangha friends, and one of their partners, much fitter and quite a bit younger than me, lovingly acted as my 'sherpas' on the trail. They retrieved my water from the pack, when I needed it, and urged me on with love and encouragement when I wanted to quit.

After four and a half hours, we made it to the summit. We huddled together in the mist and wind and had our photo shoot, snapped by my friend's partner, who had the courage to remove his gloves to take the picture for us. The seagull stood on a step near us, walking sideways to anchor himself.

We made it to the top. We raised over £700 for the Stan Kukalowicz Bursary Fund. We overcame the most adverse conditions to complete our harrowing journey. I couldn't have done it without my friends.

This hike to the top of Mount Snowdon was a sort of mirror of my grief journey, this year. I have kept moving, with one foot in front of the other, when I wanted to quit. I have had times when I could not see what was in front of me and I have had to keep my head down and press on. I have climbed through the most difficult conditions, and I have had the support and loving kindness of friends to help me through it.

I have made it through my first year. I have made it to the top.

Grief Like A River

For the past few weeks, I have become weary of this grief. It's not that I want to deny or forget my husband. I am still talking to him and kissing his photo in the mornings. I still think of him many times throughout the day and remember his words and his mannerisms and the unique way he walked down the hill toward the car. It is just that the weight of grieving is so exhausting and relentless that, sometimes, it feels good to turn toward something else. My grief has felt, lately, like I am trudging up a steep path with a sack full of rocks upon my back. These days, I am still trudging up the path. But I have wanted to set aside that bag of rocks for a while.

Turning toward other things in my life has meant that I have spent less time reading grief blogs and articles on the internet. I have not focused on reading, writing and responding to posts in my Writing Your Grief alumni support group. I have spent less time thinking about and preparing posts for this blog.

I don't know if this means that I am avoiding my grief. Perhaps that is the case. But perhaps it is healthy to set it aside, now and then. I know that the grieving will return. It will trickle into my consciousness at times and at other times it will flow like an angry river, overtaking me. I do not intend to block its flow through my life. The grief will always be there, in one form or another, waiting patiently for me to move into its current.

Yesterday was Father's Day, and I thought about Stan and the father that he was, and remembered some of the stories his children told me. Stan became a father at 17 years of age. He married and had three more children, in quick succession, with the woman he described as his first love. They divorced when their youngest child, Gavin, was very small, but Stan did his best to provide for them, bringing them to his small flats for weekend visits, taking them on holidays in the countryside, sharing love and warmth and advice from that generous heart of his.

Later, when he was in his 40s, and his other children were almost grown, he and his second wife had two boys. They experienced a different father from the young, struggling Stan the older children knew. Their father was a Senior Manager in local government. He worked long hours under a great deal of stress, but he had the money to provide for them in a different way than he had been able to do with his older kids. They, too, have shared fond memories of him, how he came to visit them after they moved with their mother to Scotland, how he drove that long drive, several times a year, to see them, no matter the weather, how he taught them about music and politics and compassion and joy.

Last year, Father's Day came only two weeks after Stan's tragic death. I don't think any of us even remember it. But this year, it must have been a very hard day for his children. Their father died so young. He was 63. One of them just graduated from University, recently, and his father was not there to see it. His grandchildren are growing up without him. There is a hole in all of their lives, now, that he once filled.

I grieve for my husband, as his widow, and I cannot understand, fully, what it is like for them to have lost their dad in the way that they did. But I do have an inkling of what means to lose a father who was so young. My father was 62 when he died, only a year younger than Stan, and I was 30 years of age, and pregnant, when he passed away, after an eighteen-month battle with lung cancer. He didn't get to meet my son. I didn't have him to lean on when I was sad or struggling with taking on the responsibilities of motherhood. He didn't get to see me get married, or graduate from University with a Master's Degree.

He died in 1987, almost 28 years ago, now.

He lived life unconventionally, and he reminded me, in many ways, of my Stan. He taught me about caring for others and he had a philosophical and spiritual perspective on the world that I carry with me, today. I still have a couple of letters he sent me, through the post (remember those?), when I was living in Mexico. I take them out and read them from time to time, these written expressions of the man that I cherished.

Yesterday, I grieved for them both. I grieved for Stan, my beloved husband, and for the father that he was to his children, and for the place he can no longer fill in their lives. I grieved for my own father, too.

So I know that this grief is not going anywhere, and perhaps it is alright for me to take a break from it. My sack of grief rocks is there for me to pick up again, when I am ready. It contains the remnants of all my losses, sweet memories of them all, and what they meant to me, the holes in my life that were once filled with their presence.

I know, now, that grief never truly leaves us. It is not something to get over or work through. It will always be with us, no matter how long our loved ones have been gone. It weaves itself into our hearts, and becomes a part of the textured fabric of our lives.

Today, I remember Stan, the father. I remember my father, too. Happy Father's Day to them both, wherever they are.

Gone Too Soon.

Without Him In It

This week marked another anniversary in the long and winding journey without my husband—his 65th birthday, on July the 2nd. Last year, his birthday came less than a month after he died, and I can't say I even remember it. I had returned to work the day before, and I must have walked through my day in that office like a zombie on auto-pilot, still numb from the shock of his sudden passing.

An entire year has ensued, without him in it.

When I think of the cruel twist of fate that brought us together for such a short time, then swept him away from me in an instant, my anger rises, and sometimes I let it carry me away. I get lost in the injustice of it. I shake my fist at the skies. If I believed that there was a God with a plan, I would be cursing him. Instead I cry out to Stan, asking him why he left us in the way that he did—as if he deliberately chose to wreak this havoc on all of our lives.

Sometimes grief does not conform to our sense of propriety. Sometimes there is no logic in it. Sometimes we have to let it erupt, so that we can move through it.

Yet I know that I am not the only one who has loved and lost. All of our stories are tragic. Those who spent a lifetime with their partners feel cheated, too. Those who watched their partners wither away with a terminal illness must feel angry, too, having to witness their loved one's pain, helpless to ease their suffering.

Our grief journeys are so personal and intimate that it is tempting, sometimes, to compare the depth of our grief and the tragedy of our loss to that of others. But there is no hierarchy to this grief. Our loved ones have vanished, and we are without them, and there is no easy way to cut through this pain. We have to live it, and share it, and remember we are not alone in it.

On the day he died, Stan stood at the altar of the chapel and read a moving tribute he had written for his beloved son, Gavin. He talked about his charm and wit, and about the struggles he had weathered in his short life. Then, he stopped, and gathered himself. He told us that he knew he was not the only one who had faced a loss. He asked us all to pause for a moment, in silence, and remember the people we knew who may be grieving the death of someone they loved.

When I want to turn inward in my sorrow, and nurture my sense of injustice, I remember him, standing there, in his darkest hour, reaching out to the people around him. In the midst of his deepest pain, my husband showed compassion.

It has been more than a year since he left us. We have spent two of his birthdays without him. To mark his day, I hiked to the top of the hill where we spread his ashes. I planted a buddleia there, on the 9th of June, the anniversary of his death. But it is cold and windy on the summit, not a nurturing environment for new growth, and I was afraid the plant might have perished.

The day before his birthday was the hottest July day on record, here in England, but this day was cool and breezy, with a light cloud cover. My path to his spot on the hill was lined with the vibrant colour of wildflowers, glowing in purples, yellows, and reds. As I rounded the path to the top, I prepared for the fact that the buddleia I planted may not have survived, and I told myself it would be alright if it hadn't. Still I searched for some sign of it as soon as I reached the summit.

The buddleia is still there. It is a bit scraggly, but it has taken root, and its buds will soon bloom into delicate, cone shaped flowers. I was so happy to see it, its hardy leaves waving in the winds, its roots nestled in amongst the heather.

That scraggly plant reminds me of myself. I have weathered the storms and sorrows of an entire year without the man with whom I had planned to grow old. I have taken root in a place that is foreign to me, a place that did not feel like much of a home, initially, without him in it.

I hope I can continue to grow and flourish in this place that he loved, and that I can reach out to others in the way that he did, even when it is difficult and dark and I want to turn inward.

I try to keep his memory alive with plants, and hikes, and words on the page.

But I know that it is through sharing the depth and the breadth of his kindness that I can truly honour his spirit.

Enough

This photo was taken a year ago, on the 12th of July, and came up on my FB page as a 'memory'. I hate those memory posts. They are a stark reminder of the sadness and turmoil of this past year, as I have wandered through the days without my husband. But this one was shocking to me. It is a photo of some rocks, near my home, called Worm Stones, and I had apparently hiked up to them, just one month after his death.

I wondered how I managed to do that. How did I take myself on a hike only a month after he collapsed and died, right in front of me? How have I managed to do all the things I have done, this year?

I have kept myself busy. Too busy. I have been on four retreats in the UK, visited Ireland and an animal sanctuary in Spain, and gone on several weekend visits to his favourite places. I have returned home to America for Thanksgiving, and visited friends and family, there. I have hiked miles into the hills and climbed a mountain with my friends.

Most recently, I have been working on the house. I have pulled up the carpet and have now, through the kindness of one of Stan's friends, had my walls painted. I have rearranged and minimised his art pieces, and made my house more spacious. I have let go of my television.

In many ways, this year, I have faced the reality of my grief head on. There has been no other way around it. But in some ways, I have used all this activity to avoid the loneliness and sorrow. I have not settled into the now of my new existence. Instead, I have organised my thoughts and spent my days preparing for the next trip, activity, or task. I have kept my mind cluttered with preparations for the future.

But now I have the house the way I want it, and there is only a little more to do. I have to conserve my funds, so will be taking fewer trips to places. I will not be visiting America until sometime next year, and perhaps I won't be able to do so, then, either. I no longer have the comforting noise of television to blunt the deafening silence. I have no more plans to make for the immediate future. I must sit with what is happening in my life, right here. Right now.

This is a frightening prospect. I have always been a planner. Even in my daily meditation, my first few minutes are consumed with plans for later in the day, tomorrow, next weekend, a few months from now. It takes me longer than most people, I think, to settle.

It's not that planning for the future is a negative thing, necessarily. It is just that all these plans and preparations distract me from seeing what is real for me, today.

So, this weekend, I tried to do that. I tried to sit with, and reflect upon, my current circumstances. The silence that surrounded me was calm and peaceful. And it allowed the sadness of my many losses to arise.

I thought about my mother, and remembered some scenes from our last few months together, when she was so vulnerable, and needed my help, but was afraid to ask for it. I remembered her face when she told me she wasn't sure she had the strength to get better, or if she even wanted to. I remembered my sister, so happy to see me, one day, after her surgery, her toothless grin as she asked me to feed her some Jello.

I thought of my Stan. I think of him daily, but, with the silence, the images of our life together became more clear and present. I could almost hear his footsteps on our steep staircase, as he took them, one by one, holding on to the rail, in the mornings. I had a laugh at his funny sayings, the way he mangled simple words with no apologies, and no attempts to pronounce them correctly. I remembered how he greeted me in the mornings, when he awakened, so happy to be alive and in this world another day. I felt the sadness but I was not overwhelmed by it. I noticed it, and allowed it.

I read a book and studied my dharma teachings, and meditated and did my yoga practice. I walked a bit in these hills. I didn't think much about the future.

My life without Stan is not how I planned it. I wanted to grow old with him. I hoped we would have many more years together. But he's gone, and I can't bring him back. I can only bring the love I had for him into my present. I can only carry the warmth and kindness of his expansive spirit into the life that I have, now. It's not a bad life. It is rich with the beauty of these hills and the love of family and friends, with books and teachings and words and art. It would have been so much richer with him in it. But it is the life I have, and I have to live it.

This life I have, it has to be enough. Without my constant searching for the next project or trip or task to make myself feel more purposeful and complete. Without the constant distraction and intoxication of television and internet. Without the comfort and sedation of too much food and sugar. Just this. This day.

Enough.

Walking The Path Where The Ghost Cows Live

It is the middle of August, and it feels as if the warmth of summer has left us, though we never really had a summer, here in England, this year. Already the air is ripe with the smell of harvest: the spiky, purple thistle flowers have morphed into white milk pods, their silky seeds floating into the sky with the slightest hint of wind, the sloping green hills are slowly giving way to the purple bloom of heather, and the blackberry flowers have popped into green and red buds. Soon, they will turn black, and be ready for picking, their berries succulent and sweet.

I walk the rocky path past the white cows who lounge amongst the green grass that feeds them. They are a rare sight, these albino creatures. Sometimes they feed in the valley, near the gurgling creek at the bottom of the path, but today they linger by the stone wall at the top. I remember seeing them on my walk the day after my husband died. I stared at them for hours, that day, and they stared back at me, as if within their brown eyes lurked a kind of knowing, a willingness to share my sorrows. I have loved them ever since.

I call them ghost cows, because they are white, and seem ethereal, and around them there is a mist of another realm. Their presence brings me comfort, and I search for them, whenever I walk these hills.

I am settling into this life without him. I have slowed my life down to a crawl. I am working only three days a week, and I am home on most of the other ones, where I am learning to sit with, rather than run from, this loss. I have let go of the noise and distractions that kept me from the reality of his death, and the truth of his absence. I am learning to sit with the knowledge that I am alone.

They say that we continue a relationship with our beloveds, even after their deaths, and that our relationship with them deepens, though they are no longer at our sides, and I have found this to be true. My time with my husband was so fleeting that we barely had the chance to grow into one another's lives. I am jealous of those who knew him for years, for decades, for his entire life. I only got a tiny glimpse of him before he was taken from me, and sometimes I feel that glimpse fading with the winds.

Recently I have been asking him and myself if our relationship was as real and as rich and as deep as I claim. I have always been prone to fantasy. When I was a child, I had, not one, but five, imaginary friends. They lived in my garage and carried distinct personalities and names. When I was old enough to go to school, my sister told me I was too big for them, so I coordinated an elaborate funeral, and buried them in the woods near our house. My fantasy world seemed so much better than the real world I inhabited, then. And, through the years, my imagination has served me well, and been a source of solace, an aid to help me cope.

So I wonder, was our love just a dream? Have I idealised the depth of our love for one another, made it sentimental and sweet, robbed it of its truth? Did he love me as much as I like to think? Would we have still been together ten years from now, had I not lost him to this tragic death? Or would he drift away, like the others, finding my mood swings and eccentricities too much for him to bear?

Our romance will be forever preserved, in the threads of my memory, through the filter of my perception. What if it was not as I remember? How can I sift through these filters to find the truth?

I know this—my love for him was real—as real as anything I have ever known or felt, and perhaps will ever know again. And those who knew him say I made him happy, and that he seemed brighter, and calmer, in the last few years of his life, the life we shared, and that our love made him a better and more peaceful man. I want to hold on to this. I want to weave their assurances into my thread of memory, and I want to believe that, had he lived, we would have grown old together, resting in the comfort of each other's arms.

I stand at the fence and talk to the ghost cows. I look into their deep, knowing eyes. Walkers pass me on the path, and give me a wide berth. Perhaps they think me a bit mad. Perhaps they want to leave me to it. I've given up the desire to please others, or to care what people think. Life is short, and in a minute, it is finished, and as long as I am able, I want to drink it in.

I'll carry my husband with me, down this path, where the ghost cows live. I'll talk to them, and to him, until the need to do so has vanished. I'll hold on to the memory of our love, and trust in its truth. It is this thread of memory to which I'll cling, this thread that gives me strength, and succour, and, some days, a sliver of hope.

Back When My Heart Was Pure

In the beginning, in the first edges of my grief, my heart felt like an open wound, and in the midst of the pain and shock of those first few days and months after the death of my husband, there was little I could do to close it.

My heart was open to the world. I didn't have the energy or the wherewithal to shut it down, to protect it, to close the door on it. My heart was broken open and all the pain and love that I carried for him seeped out into the universe.

Gone was my customary shyness. I needed and accepted the kindness and embrace of those who knew of my sorrow. I spent more time in the company of others. In the early days, the scales were taken from my eyes, and I saw with such clarity the tenuousness of the life all around us. I had no shield from this truth. It was with me in every moment.

Something happens when a loved one is lost, particularly if the loss is sudden and unexpected. In an instant, we let go of all that we once held true: any certainty about our stability on this planet, the delusion that we have some kind of control, the idea that whatever we hold dear is going to last. All of the beliefs that keep us grounded in this life are shattered, and suddenly, there is no solid ground on which to stand.

It is a terrifying place to be, this place without grounding.

That fear can move us in many directions. Some people shut down in the face of it. Some people hide and go within. Others fall into depression and despair.

Me? I became wide open for a while. I held my heart in my hands. I shared the depths of my pain without filter. I held onto those around me and let them lift me up. I told more people I loved them. I lost my fear of rejection. It didn't matter, then, what I received in return. I wanted those around me to know how much I cared. I wanted them to know that they mattered. I didn't wait for a response. I didn't need one.

That was in the beginning, in the early months of my grief, when the knowledge of death was fresh and immediate and raw.

But it has been a few months, now, 14, to be exact, and in those months, my grief has lost its sore and seeping edge. I have covered over the open wound. I have found my filter again. I have wrapped my heart in a blanket. I have become more careful with my feelings. I do not share in the way I used to.

Perhaps this is a necessary step. Perhaps it is not reasonable or helpful to walk around with an open wound. But I don't want to lose this edge, completely. I don't want to return to my melancholic, isolated self, who was reticent with others, afraid to reach toward them, letting the possibility of rejection keep me from expressing my love.

This weekend, I drove to the beautiful moors in North Yorkshire, near Whitby, saw a friend's brilliant performance in a play, met up with another friend, and walked amongst the blooming heather in the hills. This is not something I would have considered, in my previous life, before the death of my beloved. I would have hesitated. I would have thought my presence an inconvenience, at best, an intrusion into someone's schedule, only tolerated out of politeness.

I am so glad I made the trip. I delighted in seeing her, up there, on the stage, and I was happy I was there to show my support and appreciation of her. I loved visiting with my other friend, who has been away with her family during the holidays, and who I have not seen for weeks. The walk through the moors was stunningly beautiful, a feast for the senses, and I loved sharing it with my friend.

My heart is not as open as it was in the first few weeks and months of my grief. I don't experience the deep lows and wrenching pain that was so much a part of those early days. I have fewer moments of soaring joys and great insight that early edge brought me, as well.

Most days I am somewhere in the middle, and perhaps that is as it should be. Perhaps it is good to protect ourselves a bit. Riding that roller coaster of emotion and passion is exhausting.

I have not lost my edge, completely. I am acutely aware of the temporary nature of all things around me, able to reach toward others from time to time, always sitting with the ever-present knowledge of his absence, an empty place that cannot or perhaps should not be filled. It is where he belongs, in me. It is my memory. It is how I keep him with me, alongside me in this journey.

I don't want to claim that this experience has changed me for the better. I won't be one of those people who so superficially finds 'the blessing' in an experience like this. Losing my husband in this way was horrible. His loss has created a great void. His absence from this world is a tragedy. I would not wish this on anyone. I would give anything to not have had to go through it. I would give anything to have him here, with me, his wide, generous heart intertwining with mine, opening me, little by little.

But it has changed me. I will never be the old Tricia, again. I don't know if that is a good or a bad thing. Perhaps I don't need to put a value on it.

It just is.

Autumn

Embracing the Silence

As I write this blog post, I am preparing for a ten day, silent retreat at a women's Buddhist retreat centre a few hours south of my home. I will be offline and encouraged to set aside all reading and writing devices for the entire retreat. The thought of this, I must admit, is a bit terrifying. I am well acquainted with being on my own and not talking much. I prefer silence to idle chatter. However, I do not go anywhere without a book or two, a magazine, my journal, and various pens and writing implements.

Writing and reading are my coping tools. I have used them since I was a child. I remember waiting with anticipation for the bookmobile to come around my neighbourhood in the summer. I learned to read when I was five years old, and from that young age, I consumed books like candy. They helped me learn about families and worlds far beyond my own, and I was soothed by the notion that other children struggled with issues and overcame seemingly insurmountable obstacles, too.

My husband was often confounded by my need to carry a load of books with me, wherever we went, even if it was only a short drive into the hills. I did not always use them, but I had to have them with me. At night I would bring a book or my Kindle to bed. This was an issue for us, as he could not sleep with any sort of light in the room, and I needed to be able to read myself to sleep. When he went upstairs to bed, he put his head on the pillow, and went to sleep. It seemed so simple to him. He did not suffer from insomnia or from anxiety around bedtime, as I did, and do, even more so, now that I have this life without him.

A few weeks ago, I wrote a blog post that was a sort of story in third person about a woman who brings her I Pad, other reading, and a snack upstairs to bed with her. Putting my bedtime rituals onto the page helped me to see that I needed to look at how I was choosing to soothe myself, and avoid the fact of my aloneness, particularly around bedtime. I began, after that, to gently try to change my approach, and tried leaving my electronic devices and snacks downstairs. I continued, however, to allow myself a novel or magazine.

I found that, as with many things, the fear of coming to bed without my coping tools was much greater than the reality. I was able to read a bit, then fall asleep, and my sleep felt deeper, and more natural. When I awakened in the night, as I often do, I was able to, most nights, return to sleep without having to read. I tried to just lie in bed and listen to my breathing, instead.

But now, for ten days, I am asked to put even these small comforts aside. I am asked to try to sit with the silence and not 'do' anything, to set aside words and let my mind rest.

Perhaps this is what I am afraid of. Perhaps it is this that terrifies me the most--the things that may arise when my mind is at rest.

At home, when I sit for meditation, the sadness often wells up in me, from a deep place within, and I erupt into sobs. In the beginning, this happened every time I tried to sit, and for several weeks after Stan's death, I could not bear to meditate, as the sorrow it brought to the surface was just too great. But now, most days, I am able to sit for 30 or 40 minutes without crying. I am able to feel the sadness, which is always there, and let it pass.

But I wonder how will it be for me, when I have no buffers for this sadness? When I sit for six hours in meditation throughout the day, with nothing to soothe the sorrow, in between?

As the time for my retreat grows near, the fear of those long days without the comfort of words on the page, whether reading or writing them, increases.

This embracing of silence is not for the weak of heart. It is a big step. It is asking me to take off the blanket I have wrapped around me, to see me through the dark times, since I was a little girl.

I know that my husband would be very proud of me for stepping into this silence in a way I have never done before. I know that he would be applauding the efforts I have made, in the last few weeks and months, to set aside all of the compulsive habits I have used for so long, habits that soothe but also deaden me: television, long hours on the internet, and now, for a short while (not forever, I must remind myself), the comfort of words on the page.

I hope it will give me the space I need to grow, and that it will help me to turn loose of some of the habits I have developed, through the years, that hinder my growth.

I hope it will help me get clear.

Living On Memory Lane

For ten days, at a retreat centre in Shropshire, I put away my books, pens, and paper, and embraced the quiet. I did not rush to scribble down each passing thought. I did not seek the distraction and comfort of the books that called to me. I sat with what came, and let it flow through me. In that spacious and quiet place, I learned to set aside my well-worn stories about myself and the world.

We arrived at Taraloka, a Buddhist Retreat Centre built by, run by, and designed for, women, at 4 p.m. on a Thursday afternoon. We were the first ones there, and I used the time to settle into my room and become accustomed to the silence. Our first evening brought the arrival of 24 other women, a leisurely dinner, and a meditation, before we all wandered off to our rooms for an early night of rest. Our next 9 days would begin at 6 a.m.

Though the initial two days were talking days, I found this time without the written word to be excruciatingly painful. Without the easy comfort of internet, books, and writing, the images of my husband, all the memories of our life together, and the tragic story of his death, poured through me. A well of sadness erupted from deep within, and I cried. And cried. And cried. I cried for the first two days.

And then, it shifted. Allowing time for things to move through me brought me to a different place.

Walking down the long path at Taraloka, one morning, after a deep meditation, I lifted my head and noticed the beauty all around me. I marvelled at the hay bales, recently cut and shaped into large cylinders. I saw the intricate threads of spider webs draped across nettle plants, the morning dew drops clinging to them. I felt the sun warm its way through the mist. And I felt my husband's spirit encircle me.

Before that morning, I would go for long walks in the countryside, and each sight, smell or sound would bring forth a memory of Stan. I would see a beautiful flower and remember the time I sent him pictures of flowers from my phone, and he texted me back the names of all of them. Then I would chase that memory with another memory. I'd remember the time we stopped at the top of a hillside in Scotland, and it was ablaze with orange and yellow and purple wildflowers, and we sat in the car together, in silent awe of them. I'd remember the time he drove me through our neighbourhood, hunting for lilacs, my favourite flower.

After that, another memory. And then another. And another.

Before I knew it, I'd be awash in memory, and filled with the pain of his absence. Gone was the beauty of that present moment. All I could see, then, was the loss of him.

Standing on that gravel path, I recognised that I have been clinging to those memories of him and of us like a drowning rat on a sinking raft. I thought that I could only hang on to him through memory. To move from those memories was too frightening to consider. It felt like a betrayal of him. I was so afraid I would forget.

I saw that I have spent the last year of my life camped out on Memory Lane.

But on that sweet morning at Taraloka, I kept my feet and heart rooted in the present. I had a memory or two, but I let them go, instead of clinging to them, and gently brought my attention back to the rich world unfolding around me: the wild geese, flying through the mist in perfect formation, the cows, noisily chewing their grass, the smell of damp hay, the feel of the gravel beneath my feet. I stayed with the moment, and I felt his presence. He felt as close to me as my breath.

I realised I did not have to live on Memory Lane to keep my beloved husband in my heart. I saw that I could bring him alongside me on this journey through my life, as it is, today. It is not the life I had planned or wanted. But it is the life I have.

And memories fade with time. It is no use clinging to them.

When he was alive, he tried to help me see the joy of inhabiting this planet. But I was too wound up and anxious to truly understand what he was trying to teach me. My life has always been cloaked with a layer of melancholy, a veil of sorrow that even meeting and loving him could not entirely erase.

For some reason, that veil has been lifted. Perhaps it is his last gift to me. This gift of the present. This knowing. This sense of belonging. This peace.

I will still take a stroll down Memory Lane, from time to time, recalling the stories of our life together. I will laugh at his adorable and endearing ways. But my husband knew the value of the present. He delighted in living. And I know he would want that for me, too.

It is not that the pain of losing him has vanished. There is no 'moving on' from this grief, completely. Just yesterday, I sat with others in my grief writing group, and, as I read something I had written about missing him, I let my tears fall.

But now, I can carry this grief alongside the joy that can be found in this life I am living. I can be filled with gratitude for having known him. For getting to share a bit of time with him on this planet. For having met a man who had such wisdom, such kindness, and so much love to give.

I can visit Memory Lane, but I no longer have to live there.

As I step foot into the world of the present, I feel his big, wide arms surrounding me.

Pockets of Loss

My mind and heart feel a bit scattered, this week. I have returned from retreat to work and errands and the ups and downs that characterise life in the real world. Each time I go on a retreat, I want to stay there, where there is space and quiet and a relief from worry about finances and obligations and commuting and cleaning and all the things that we resist and resent. But I know that living the life of a monk or a hermit is not my path, however appealing it seems, at times. So I return, and try to juggle the mundane tasks of life in western society with the contemplative life that calls to me.

I am facing some possible changes at work, where there are huge budget cuts expected, in the next two years, which could mean that the program I am managing will end. This means more changes in my work life, and, though I don't have a lot of fear around finding a job (there are always jobs in the field of child abuse and neglect, unfortunately), I am not ecstatic about the prospect of having to acclimate to a new work environment. I would prefer to move from this position to retirement, but I am fortunate to even have a job, in these economic times, and for that I am grateful.

My husband's granddaughter is headed toward University today, and we all gathered at his daughter's house, on Friday, to send her off and wish her well. I felt Stan's presence all around us. I could picture him, sitting on the sofa, in his usual spot, at his daughter's house, beaming with pride, with me there, right beside him. We were all mindful of his physical absence, that night, as we raised our glasses in toast to her, and to her accomplishments.

My nephew is coming for a short visit, today. He grew up in Indiana, and now lives in Denver, and loves hiking and rocks, having studied geology, so I hope to show him some of our beautiful countryside while he is here. He lost his older brother, who died at the age of 23, in 2004. Eleven years ago. Chris' death was a shock to us all, a devastating loss for our family, and for his father, him, and his sister, especially. It is hard to believe that someone can die so very young. I am mindful of this loss, and of the hole it left in all of our lives, as I ponder going to meet my nephew at the train station this afternoon.

And I am remembering my father, today. He died on the 1st of October in 1987. 28 years ago. He was 62. I remember, then, thinking that he was old, not old enough to die, but that he had lived a life that was long and full. Now, at the age of 58, I see how very young 62 is. He missed out on so much of our lives, and of his. He always talked about wanting to live to see the year 2000. He didn't get to do that. He didn't get to meet my son, a boy he would have loved and celebrated and with whom he would have found great commonality.

It feels strange, sometimes, to think back to the days when my dad was alive. I was so close to him, and I relied on him for his wisdom and knowing and for his emotional support when I was struggling with the dramas that we create for ourselves in adolescence and early adulthood. He always knew the right words to say to help me get a perspective on my often self-imposed suffering. He understood what was important in life, and he tried to help me see it.

I remember accompanying him to a radiation treatment when he was fighting lung cancer, in the summer of 1986. Watching him take off his shirt and lie under that big machine, I saw him as vulnerable for the first time in my life. His body looked so small and frail. I knew, in that moment, that it would only be a matter of time before he left us, and the thought of losing him was almost too much for my heart to bear.

We didn't get that time to ponder the loss of my husband. He died at the age of 63, and witnessing his sudden death was a trauma of its own that has complicated our grief journeys. One moment, his strong presence was a source of comfort and solace for us, and the next moment, he was gone.

Sometimes, I feel overwhelmed by all these pockets of loss.

When I was on retreat, I walked, most mornings, to the old church down the road, and strolled amongst the graves of the people who once lived in the village nearby. I love graveyards. I am a storyteller, and I love to read the short stories of peoples' lives and deaths, etched so poignantly into the stone.

There were graves of infants and children, of brothers and sisters, and graves of husbands who died, and their wives, buried next to them, twenty years later. At the turn of the century, five children fell through broken ice on a pond near the village, and all of them drowned. Each day, I would trace my finger along the names of those children. Eight years old. Ten years old. Nineteen. Sixteen. Twenty.

I found comfort there, sitting among the graves. It helped me, not to minimise my losses, or discount them, but to remember that others had experienced so much loss, too. It helped me to remember that loss is inevitable, and that the only way to protect ourselves from it is to hide from love, and from life, to harden, to build a wall between ourselves and others, to shrivel up inside.

As painful as I find them, these pockets of loss are important, and necessary. They mean that I am still soft, and alive, and that my heart remains open to the world that unfolds around me.

There is so much pain. And so much beauty.

As much as it hurts, I am grateful for these pockets of loss. I am grateful to have known my dad, so full of humour and wisdom, to have known my nephew, that chubby, ginger haired boy, to have lived all those years with my mother, my sister, my sister in law. To have known Gavin, Stan's son, who died two weeks before Stan. To have lived those short, sweet, three years with my husband.

To have known him. To have known them all.

To have loved.

Searching For Stan

It is a chilly October morning and I am listening to the wind and watching the early light steal across the sky. I want to write words that are meaningful and resonate with others who are grieving, too. I want to speak to the parts of me that others may keep hidden, even from themselves. I want to share the broken bits and the light of hope that shines between the cracks in the brokenness. I want to be eloquent and wise.

But some days, the words aren't there. Some days all I can do is speak of my direct experience with grief and loss. Some days all I can do is write what is present for me, in this moment, and hope that the words make sense.

It has been an exhausting week, though I didn't seem to accomplish much. Recently, the expectations at my workplace have made me question my capability for the job and even my desire to remain in the field in which I have worked for the past 35 years. And I have found myself searching for Stan, in the hope that he could, as he did when he was alive, ground me in the truth, help me shift my thinking and priorities, and gain a wider perspective.

But I don't know where he is.

Since he died, 15 months ago, I have searched for him, everywhere.

I have tried to find him in my memory, pouring over photos and preserving on the page the tiny details of our life together. I have travelled miles to visit the places that he loved, and showed me, and that I grew to love, too. I have shared memories with his friends and children. I have tried to paint a picture with my words for those who did not know him, regaling them with stories of his antics, his humour, his wisdom and character. I have tried to teach them, through my words, about the man that he was.

I have wrapped my arms around myself and tried to remember the warmth of his touch. I have kept his dressing gown and his winter hat that hold within them the traces of his scent. I have kept his wallet, his glasses, his nail clippers, the soaps he used the last morning of his life.

I have walked these hills and talked to him, and searched for his beloved rabbits in the grasses, hoping they would bring me a sign from another realm--the realm where he may be resting.

I want to believe that he still exists, somewhere, and that, if I try hard enough, and if I am good enough, I will find him.

Some days, he feels as close to me as my skin. Some nights, when I lie in bed, I can feel the weight of his arms around me, and his kiss upon my cheek as I drift off to sleep.

But other days, it's as if he has vanished into thin air.

There are those who believe in heaven, and an afterlife, and are comforted by the knowing that they will visit their loved ones when they die, that the husbands, wives, parents and children who have passed before them will be standing in the mist, bathed in white light, beckoning them to come, to join them, in a place of eternal peace.

I want to believe that, too.

There are those who believe that we continue, when we die, but not as ourselves, that there is no fixed soul that travels to a great beyond, but that our lives are like a flame, and that a piece of us continues and becomes a part of All That Is.

This is the belief that makes sense for me, today, sitting here, watching the green and orange leaves dance with the wind.

I don't know what the afterlife holds. I only know that I cannot visit it, now. That wherever Stan is, whatever he has become, he is not the Stan I knew and loved, here, on this earth. That I can't reach for him in the way that I want to, can't rely on him to make my world kinder and safer, that I can't nestle into his arms and know that I am going to be alright.

Since he died, so many months ago, now, my heart has been filled with so much longing.

Perhaps it is time to put this longing to rest. It doesn't serve me, or him, wherever he is, to continue to cling to the hope of finding what can no longer be.

Perhaps I can sit with the knowledge that Stan lives in me--in the way he changed me, helped me to learn, and discover, and grow.

Sitting here, watching the morning light dimmed by a soft layer of cloud, I know that there are no concrete answers. There is only the mystery. There is only the knowledge of the thin veil between life and death that brings meaning and sweetness to our time here on earth. There is no certainty. Only more questions.

My search for Stan is not finished. I will look for him again. And maybe my longing can never be fully put to rest. There will always be a part of my heart that wants him back, standing before me, the way he was, that will wish for what can never be again.

It's what makes us human, this longing. This searching. This ever present and never diminishing love.

The Things We Carry

"They shared the weight of memory. They took up what others could no longer bear. Often, they carried each other, the wounded or weak." from The Things They Carried by Tim O'Brien

This quote is from a story by Tim O'Brien about men who were in the Vietnam war. It is a classic story that speaks to the universal themes of memory and loss. As I reflect upon the year of writing that I have shared with you, and this, my last blog post as Monday's Writer for Widow's Voice, I am moved by these words.

In this blog, and as members of a community for which no one wants to qualify, we carry each other. We lift each other up and bear witness to the things that others can't stand to see. We carry each other through the most difficult and terrifying moments of our lives.

We sit with each other in silence when there are no easy words or platitudes to fix our sorrows. We stand together, as different as we are, in age, ethnicity, status, and country of origin, and help each other navigate this bewildering landscape of grief.

We know that the people 'out there', who have not seen what we've seen, cannot begin to understand what sits so solidly in our minds and hearts: that there is so much pain, and so much beauty; that we grieve because we loved; that we don't know how we are going to get through each day, but that, somehow, for some reason, we are still here; that gradually, so slowly, we begin to enter into the world of the living again, but that we will never 'get over' this loss; that we carry them with us, and will continue to carry them, for the rest of our days.

Writing here has helped me step through this winding and rutted path of grief. Bringing words to the page each week has kept me present and aware, when it would have been so much easier to run, to hide, to curl up into a ball and seek comfort, to numb myself from the pain of it, to become dead inside.

This blog has helped me to carry the things I would rather have set aside. And because I have learned to carry them, I can carry other things, too, into this new life without him.

I'll carry memory. I will always remember him, and keep his things around me that trigger those memories. His dressing gown still hangs on the hook of my bedroom door. I don't know when I will take it down. It is such a tender reminder of him. He wore that dressing gown every morning, wherever we were. He brought it with him on all of our trips. When he went away to retreats, he took it with him, there, too. I once bought him a fuzzy, fluffy gown, thinking it would warm him on our cold winter mornings, but he never wore it, and finally we donated it to a charity shop. Instead he wore that threadbare gown, loosely belted at the waist. Sometimes I put my face to it, still, in search of a trace of his scent.

I'll carry his spirit. Often, this year, I have felt his exuberance and humour guiding me, as I venture into new and daunting arenas. He had a love of life that I found perplexing. He had a way of encountering the world, without fear or rancour, that I loved and admired. He gifted me with an understanding of how to engage with life, and with others.

I'll carry gratitude. I witnessed the sudden and tragic death of the man that I loved, and gratitude was not a word I could have used a few months ago. I remember, early in my grief, when someone told me to be grateful for the time I had with him—if I could have reached through the internet, I would have choked her. It felt like such an insult to my sorrow. We were supposed to grow old together. We had just begun our lives. We were an older couple who had finally found a deep and abiding love, and we were looking forward to deepening it, further. How could I be grateful?

But today, I am grateful. I am so grateful that I met this man. I am grateful that he brought me here, to these gentle, windswept hills. That he brought me into his world, and shared it with me, with open arms. That he gave me this house, this village, these neighbours, this family, these friends. That he set me in the middle of his sangha too, the people who lifted me through the deep sorrow of those first few months, who held me up when I could not stand on my own.

I'll carry love—a knowledge of a real, and true, and honest love. I had a great love. So many people go through their entire lives without being able to say that. So many people are in relationships that are not real and substantive, that do not speak to the best parts of themselves, that do not help them grow and flourish, but keep them safe, and secure, and sedate, instead. Stan and I loved each other. We took risks to be together. We put aside past hurts and helped each other through fears and insecurities. We helped each other to tap into the deepest places in our hearts. We did not get much time together. But I know love because I knew him.

I'll carry hope. I could not have used that word, until recently, either. But something has shifted in my grief, and, though I am still left with the hole that often feels like a gaping wound, I carry a bit of hope, too. I have hope that I can live a life that has quality, and depth, and meaning. I have hope that I can carry his memory and his spirit into that life in a way that will honour him. I carry hope that I can use the memory of his open arms to reach out to others. I carry hope that my words will continue to speak to others in the way that they have done so, here.

These are the things I carry, and so much more: love and sorrow; Gratitude and despair; tenderness and strength.

And because of him, I carry these things, too: compassion and warmth; humour and joy; a recognition of beauty; a love of life.

I don't know how long I will remain in this world. None of us do. But I know this. Meeting and loving Stan made me a better woman. Knowing him taught me how to carry all the complexities of this life with dignity and grace. The world is a kinder, gentler, richer place, having had him in it.

I am so happy to have loved this man—Stanley Jan Kukalowicz:

2 July 1950—9 June 2014

May he rest in peace.

Epilogue: Honouring Grief; Honouring Stan

This grief journey has taught me many things—how hard it is to speak the words of grief in our western world, how we are expected to move on, rise above, solve the problem, let go—and how uncomfortable it is for those who love us to know how and what to say in the midst of such deep sorrow.

I hope that these short reflections help people who may not know how to put words to their grief. I hope it gives them permission to speak the names of the loved ones they have lost, no matter how many years have passed.

There are a few books that I would recommend to grievers:

A Grief Observed, by C.S. Lewis

Leaning Into Love, by Elaine Mansfield

The Year of Magical Thinking, by Joan Didion

The Courage to Grieve, by Judy Tatelbaum

I would also encourage those who have lost to find a support group, either online or in person. The support I have received on the internet has been invaluable to me.

For those who write, I highly recommend the Writing Your Grief workshop that is conducted online by Megan Divine. For 30 days, writers who sign up for the course receive prompts around grief and loss, and post their responses online, to share with other grieving writers in the group. As a result, a deeply close, intimate and supportive community is formed. We call it the "Tribe of After". It is an incredible group, of which I am still a part.

The web site for this workshop is listed here:

http://www.refugeingrief.com/support/30-day/

My husband believed strongly that the Dharma should be made available to all, and tried to form a bursary fund to help those who could not otherwise afford it attend retreats. It was almost ready to launch when he died. The Manchester Buddhist Centre took the money that was given in his name as a memorial to form the Stanley J. Kukalowicz Bursary Fund. It is to this fund that most of the profits of this book will be donated.

If you remember Stan, or if you have come to know him through this book, you can honour him by donating to this fund. The link to the donation page is listed below.

https://mydonate.bt.com/events/bursaryfund/181894